THEATRE OF THE FRATERNITY

**FREDERICK R. WEISMAN ART MUSEUM**

University of Minnesota
Minneapolis, Minnesota
*October 6, 1996 — January 5, 1997*

**THE KENT STATE UNIVERSITY MUSEUM**

Kent, Ohio
*February 5 — June 15, 1997*

**MUSEUM OF OUR NATIONAL HERITAGE**

Lexington, Massachusettes
*July 27, 1997 — February 1, 1998*

**UNIVERSITY ART MUSEUM**

California State University
Long Beach, California
*March 10 — April 26, 1998*

**PLAINS ART MUSEUM**

Fargo, North Dakota
*June 4 — September 6, 1998*

# THEATRE OF THE FRATERNITY

*Staging the Ritual Space*

*of the Scottish Rite of Freemasonry, 1896–1929*

Conceived and curated by

## C. LANCE BROCKMAN

*Contributions by*

Kenneth L. Ames

William D. Moore

Mary Ann Clawson

Mark C. Carnes

C. Lance Brockman

Lawrence J. Hill

*Frederick R. Weisman Art Museum*
UNIVERSITY OF MINNESOTA

Distributed by University Press of Mississippi

This book has been published

in conjunction with the exhibition

*Theatre of the Fraternity:*

*Staging the Ritual Space of the*

*Scottish Rite of Freemasonry,*

*1896–1929,* which was organized

by the Frederick R. Weisman

Art Museum and shown from

October 5, 1996, through

January 5, 1997.

The exhibition and publication
have been made possible by grants
from the National Endowment
for the Humanities and the cooperation of
the Scottish Rite Research Society.

Library of Congress
Catalog Card Number 96-085617
ISBN 0-87805-947-4

Distributed by
University Press of Mississippi
3825 Ridgewood Road
Jackson, Mississippi
39211-6492
1-800-737-7788

Edited by Susan C. Jones
Proofread by Sally Rubinstein
Designed by Jeanne Lee &
Craig Davidson
Printed in Canada
All photographs, except where
identified, were provided by the
author and Lawrence Hill.

Throughout this catalog,
text appears in a two-letter code.
This text comes from the
1959 edition of the Freemasons'
bylaws booklet, courtesy of
Duane E. Anderson. The symbols and moral lessons for the
degrees are from *To Shine in Use:
A Centennial Celebration of the
Scottish Rite Bodies of Wichita,
Kansas, 1986.* They represent the
interpretation of the ritual for
the Southern Jurisdiction, which
is currently under revision.

# contents

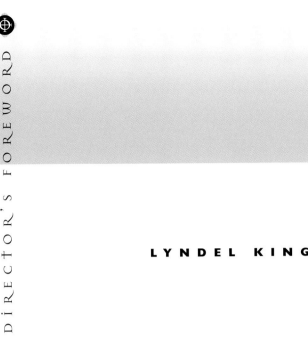

**LYNDEL KING**

THE WEISMAN ART MUSEUM IS PLEASED TO PRESENT THIS BOOK AND THE EXHIBITION IT ACCOMPANIES. This project is, in one sense, the outgrowth of a successful exhibition and catalog called *The Twin City Scenic Collection: Popular Entertainment 1895–1929*, which the Weisman (then the University Art Museum) presented in 1987 with Lance Brockman as guest curator. That project focused on turn-of-the century popular-theatre design, particularly the productions of the Twin City Scenic Company, whose archives are at the University of Minnesota. While Lance was involved with that exhibition, he became interested in the designs done for the theatrical productions that were part of fraternal organizations' initiations and that were almost unknown to scholars and the general public. Particularly impressive were those made for the Scottish Rite of Freemasonry.

Many Americans have some vague knowledge of Freemasonry or of other fraternal orders because these organizations were important parts of our parents' or grandparents' social lives in rural America, particularly in the Midwest. Still others may know of Freemasonry because eighteenth-century Austrian composer Wolfgang Amadeus Mozart was a Mason.

Freemasonry traces its origins back to medieval times, when independent artisans who moved from place to place to build castles and cathedrals established craft guilds. It remained a craft guild in Europe until the end of the sixteenth century. From this modest beginning, it developed as an international movement that promulgated fundamental moral and ethical principles not specific to any particular religion. Its rituals used allegories and symbols connected with the art of building. Freemasonry's history in the United States included George Washington and Benjamin Franklin as members.

The Masonic movement flourished in the United States from 1896 to 1929. What was the attraction? Why did so many American men join? What was so important about the theatrical productions that became part of the elaborate initiation rituals, particularly in the Scottish Rite order of Freemasonry? Was theatre significant in the increasing popularity of that order? Why? Several distinguished scholars address these and other intriguing questions in the essays that follow.

Their inquiries were funded by the National Endowment for the Humanities, which is, at this moment, embattled and fighting for its survival. This project, which will shed so much light on an important part of our shared American heritage, would not have happened without the commitment of NEH funding and the encouragement and support of its staff. Something fine in American life in the late twentieth century will be lost if we are not able to save the National Endowment for the Humanities. Our goal is to make this project exemplify the best of what the NEH partnership with institutions and individual scholars can accomplish.

As the director of the Frederick R. Weisman Art Museum at the University of

Minnesota, I am pleased the museum is able to present this interdisciplinary effort. Part of the museum's mission is to encourage interdisciplinary programs and to make the research of scholars accessible to nonspecialists. *Theatre of the Fraternity: Staging the Ritual Space of the Scottish Rite of Freemasonry, 1896–1929* represents that mission well.

The Weisman Art Museum staff must be recognized for its role in this complex undertaking. I want, especially, to thank my assistant, Gwen Sutter, for helping keep me and many details on track, as well as Colleen Sheehy, director of education; Karen Duncan, registrar; Robert Bitzan, director of public affairs; Rose Blixt, principal accountant; and Kay McGuire, our museum store manager, who handled many of the details of the publication of this book. In addition, our curator Patricia McDonnell was an important adviser, and our installation staff, headed by Mark Kramer, worked with all the consultants to ensure the smooth production of the exhibition. I want also to thank the editor, Susan Jones, who made sure all the essays helped fulfill our mission of making scholarship accessible, and the designers of this book, Jeanne Lee and Craig Davidson, whose sympathy for the material, combined with their excellent design sensibility, made this book beautiful as well as erudite. The museum also would like to acknowledge the assistance of the Masonic advisory committee and all the special project staff whom the curator, Lance Brockman, names in his acknowledgments.

The museum is grateful, most of all, to Lance Brockman, whose vision, scholarship, organization, leadership, and just plain hard work made possible the successful fruition of this book and exhibition. We are proud to present them.

I T IS A DIFFICULT TASK TO ENUMERATE ALL THOSE WHO HAVE SHARED THEIR TIME AND TALENTS IN PREPARING THIS CATALOG AND EXHIBIT. It is, however, one I undertake with pleasure and much gratitude to everyone who helped shape so much of the material to ensure the success of this project.

In preface, I must express appreciation to my wonderful students, who have listened attentively to me deviate from class lectures to discussions of fraternalism; these digressions have helped me work through many of the early concepts of this subject. I benefited from your thoughtful input on this diverse material, and I valued your constant encouragement.

I first want to acknowledge my indebtedness to Lyndel King, director of the Weisman Art Museum of the University of Minnesota, for supporting the initial ideas explored in this exhibit. She had the foresight to see the potential in this project and helped nourish, shape, and direct its many "tentacles." Second, I extend heartfelt thanks to Barbara Franco, formerly of the Minnesota Historical Society and now director of the Historical Museum of Washington, D.C. Barbara's past experience as assistant director of the Museum of Our National Heritage, which is dedicated to interpreting the fraternal movement, gave her astute insights into the material culture of nineteenth-century fraternities and female auxiliaries. She has been a valuable adviser on this project, leading me through some complicated interpretations of these rich and varied artifacts.

I am forever grateful to several members of the Masonic fraternity for your generous contributions of time and support. You found energy from your busy schedules to "fly" in the various backdrops, move scenery, rearrange properties, and adjust lighting and to share information about our "common heritage." Without you, this research would have been extremely difficult to conduct. In addition, I offer thanks to the members of the Scottish Rite Advisory Board: Forrest D. Haggard, Duane E. Anderson, S. Brent Morris, and David Board. Additional fraternal support came from C. Fred Kleinknecht, Sovereign Grand Commander of the Southern Jurisdiction. Daniel F. Levenduski and Lloyd D. Wilkerson, Sovereign Grand Inspector Generals of Minnesota and North Carolina, also worked hard on behalf of this project, providing access to Scottish Rite temples and securing sanction from the Supreme Council of the Southern Jurisdiction.

Thanks to Alan Lathrop, curator of the Performing Arts Archives of the Library of the University of Minnesota, for providing a home for the Holak and Great Western collections. Alan saw the significance of acquiring these sketches and materials to supplement the immense Twin City Scenic Collection, which was exhibited in 1987. Tom Scott, a valued alumnus of this university, solicited and contributed to the funds needed to acquire the Scottish Rite sketches; without his generous efforts, this exhibit would not have been possible.

Four museums and archives have been especially selfless with their materials and time. First, I would like to thank Tom Leavitt, director; John D. Hamilton, librarian/archivist; and Maureen Harper, registrar, at the Museum of Our National Heritage in Lexington, Massachusetts. William D. Moore, director of the Chancellor Livingston Library and Museum of the Grand Lodge of New York, has provided wonderful support in accessing artifacts and thoughtful insights in selecting images from the library's vast research resources. I would like to thank Joan Kleinknecht, librarian for the House of the Temple, Supreme Council of the Southern Jurisdiction of the Scottish Rite in Washington, D.C.; Joan unearthed many treasures that made it possible to interpret much of the exhibit. Finally, I want to express my appreciation to Harold Spelman, archivist for the Scottish Rite Bodies of Chicago.

C. Michael Volland, Volland Studios, Inc., of St. Louis; John A. Freeburg, Anoka Lodge A.F. & A.M.; Bruce C. Brockman, University of Idaho; Charles Schauss and Charles Nelson, St. Paul Lodge Number Three A.F. & A.M.; Robert L. Spangler, Jr., Little Rock Scottish Rite Bodies; Rodney M. Larson, the Grand Lodge of Minnesota; Harmon Ruliffson, Minneapolis Scottish Rite Bodies; Robert G. Davis, Guthrie Scottish Rite Bodies; Bill Peters, Minnesota Grand Lodge of the Independent Order of Odd Fellows; and John M. Myers, Wichita Scottish Rite Bodies, loaned artifacts from their personal or institutional archives and collections and provided valuable advice in interpreting seemingly dissimilar objects in the exhibit.

Special thanks to my research assistant, Wendy Waszut-Barrett, who tirelessly tracked down obscure information, organized exhibit objects, coordinated permissions for photographs, and provided scenic-art expertise for the interactive stages and the Hades scene in the exhibit. No exhibit takes place without the dedication and commitment of museum personnel and staff. This monumental undertaking was facilitated by an exceptional group of professionals who willingly shared their specialized skills. Rick Polenek served as the exhibit designer, forging a vast number of seemingly disparate objects into a cohesive whole. Kathy Stewart provided much-needed technical support and coordination. And Martin Gwinup created and engineered the interactive stages, wind machine, and structure to support the Hades scene.

Perhaps the largest debt of gratitude goes to the National Endowment for the Humanities, which issued substantial grants for both the planning symposium and the implementation of this exhibit. In the words of essayist Ken Ames, the NEH, embattled by recent budget cuts, provides the necessary support "in requiring significant humanities content in the projects that it funds; the best way to obtain NEH funding is to assemble a team of humanities scholars capable of bringing a variety of perspectives and expertise to a given project . . . The NEH can fairly claim to have altered the intellectual content of museum exhibitions in this country." (*Decorative Arts and Household Furnishings in America, 1650–1920*)

Five outstanding humanities scholars collaborated with me to share ideas and frame the issues presented in this catalog and in the exhibit; I want to express my sincere appreciation for the essays they contributed. Other scholars whose participation in the planning symposium deserves recognition include Lynn Dumenil, M. Kent Neely, and Paul Larson. A special thanks to my good friend Don Stowell, who took such an active role in this project and who, sadly, passed away in May 1995. A debt of gratitude to Kay McGuire of the Weisman Museum staff for her efforts in developing, producing, and distributing the catalog. A tremendous expression of appreciation is due to Susan Jones, who patiently edited the catalog and didactic panels; her efforts transformed the "scholarly" text into understandable and accessible prose. For graphic artists Jeanne Lee and Craig Davidson, my thanks for coordinating the "look" of the catalog and the didactic panels for the exhibit.

In addition, the United States Institute for Theatre Technology (USITT) provided, through the Edward F. Kook Endowment Fund, early support to Larry Hill, Rhett Bryson, and me so we could document much of the fraternal scenery and artifacts on display. USITT also was willing to feature this material in a scholarly forum at the national conference in Wichita, Kansas, in 1993. This exhibit, through supplemental support, will be available to members and the public, along with interpretative programming, at the USITT conference in Long Beach, California, in March 1998.

*C. Lance Brockman*

**C. LANCE BROCKMAN**

**The probable extent of the influence of secret society life may be inferred from the fact that more than 6,000,000 Americans are members of 300 such organizations, which confer about 1,000 degrees on 200,000 novitiates annually, aided, in instances, by a wealth of paraphernalia and dramatic ceremonials which rival modern stage effects.** Albert E. Stevens, *Cyclopaedia of Fraternities* (1907)

FOR MOST OF US, THE APPEAL AND SUCCESS OF THE FRATERNAL MOVEMENT IN TURN-OF-THE-CENTURY AMERICA ARE DIFFICULT TO COMPREHEND. For some, there are vague memories of, and mementos from, this all-but-lost past: ornate ribbons or lapel pins in a family member's bureau drawer, a description of a puzzling Masonic funeral service for a distant relative, peculiar symbols or iconography found on the cornerstones and cartouches of Victorian buildings, family discussions about "meeting night" at the lodge or temple. For many, of course, the most vivid image is of those "funny guys" wearing fezzes and riding motorcycles or dune buggies in civic parades.

For contemporary nonmembers, or the "profane," this kaleidoscope of imagery and fractured perceptions is the basis for our understanding why many of our relatives helped forge a "nation of joiners" at the end of the nineteenth century. To try to interpret all the social and historical influences and the layers of the myriad organizations from this time would be an exhausting task and certainly beyond the scope of this catalog. Each organization shared characteristics with others—initiations with secret rituals administered by incremental degrees, funeral services that confronted both individual and collective mortality, and elaborate hierarchical structures with exotic titles. All such secret societies were based on the older, highly successful Masonic model.

This catalog was created to accompany the exhibit "Theatre of the Fraternity: Staging the Ritual Space of the Scottish Rite of Freemasonry, 1896–1929." While providing brief, contextual discussions of the late-nineteenth-century fraternal movement, the following six essays focus specifically on the Ancient and Accepted Scottish Rite, which, at the turn of the century, adopted the full theatrical trappings of the popular-entertainment stage. The assimilation of state-of-the-art scenery, lighting, and stage effects enabled the Scottish Rite to provide new members with a dramatic initiation experience. Its success spurred the fraternity to equip existing temple spaces with theatrical trappings. And a subsequent building boom saw large fraternal stages being erected across America.

To place the Scottish Rite within the broader context of Freemasonry requires a basic understanding of the complex structure of this organization. Initiation into the "mysteries" of the first three degrees marked the beginning of Masonry for all fledgling members. And for many, this was sufficient, but a growing number of late-nineteenth-century Masons sought to pursue one or both of

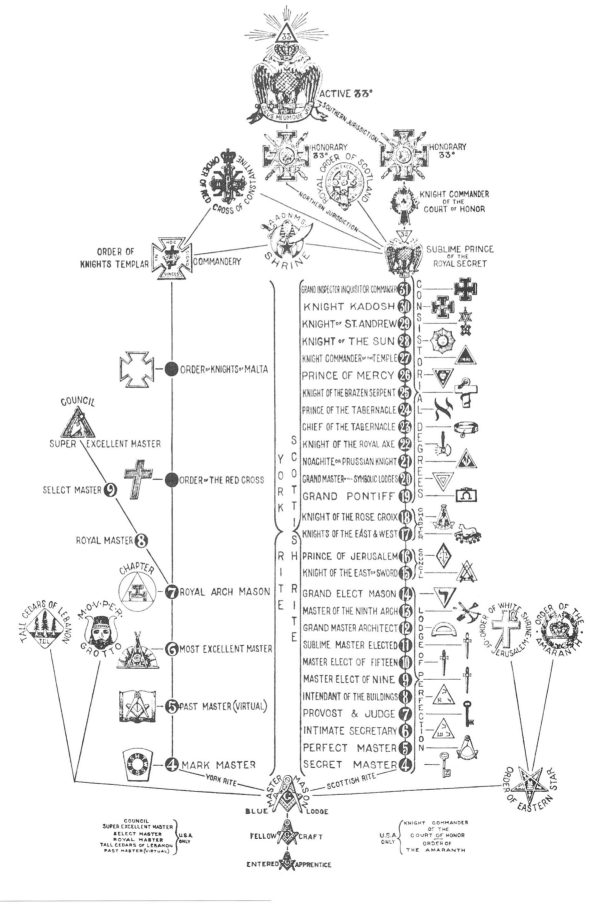

ACTIVE 33°

SOUTHERN JURISDICTION

Honorary 33° ROYAL ORDER OF SCOTLAND

NORTHERN JURISDICTION

Honorary 33°

KNIGHT COMMANDER
OF THE
COURT OF HONOR

ORDER OF RED CROSS OF CONSTANTINE

A.A.O.N.M.S.
SHRINE

SUBLIME PRINCE
OF THE
ROYAL SECRET

ORDER OF
KNIGHTS TEMPLAR    COMMANDERY

GRAND INSPECTOR INQUISITOR COMMANDER 31

KNIGHT KADOSH 30

KNIGHT OF ST. ANDREW 29

KNIGHT OF THE SUN 28

KNIGHT COMMANDER OF THE TEMPLE 27

PRINCE OF MERCY 26

KNIGHT OF THE BRAZEN SERPENT 25

PRINCE OF THE TABERNACLE 24

CHIEF OF THE TABERNACLE 23

KNIGHT OF THE ROYAL AXE 22

NOACHITE OR PRUSSIAN KNIGHT 21

GRAND MASTER OF ALL SYMBOLIC LODGES 20

GRAND PONTIFF 19

KNIGHT OF THE ROSE CROIX 18

KNIGHTS OF THE EAST & WEST 17

PRINCE OF JERUSALEM 16

KNIGHT OF THE EAST OR SWORD 15

GRAND ELECT MASON 14

MASTER OF THE NINTH ARCH 13

GRAND MASTER ARCHITECT 12

SUBLIME MASTER ELECTED 11

MASTER ELECT OF FIFTEEN 10

MASTER ELECT OF NINE 9

INTENDANT OF THE BUILDINGS 8

PROVOST & JUDGE 7

INTIMATE SECRETARY 6

PERFECT MASTER 5

SECRET MASTER 4

CONSISTORIAL DEGREES

CHAPTER

COUNCIL

LODGE OF PERFECTION

ORDER OF KNIGHTS OF MALTA

COUNCIL
SUPER EXCELLENT MASTER

SELECT MASTER 9    ORDER OF THE RED CROSS

ROYAL MASTER 8

CHAPTER

ROYAL ARCH MASON 7

YORK RITE

SCOTTISH RITE

M.O.V.P.E.R.
GROTTO

TALL CEDARS OF LEBANON
T.C.L.

MOST EXCELLENT MASTER 6

PAST MASTER (VIRTUAL) 5

MARK MASTER 4

YORK RITE          SCOTTISH RITE

MASTER MASON

BLUE          LODGE

ORDER OF WHITE SHRINE
OF JERUSALEM

ORDER OF THE
AMARANTH

ORDER OF EASTERN STAR

COUNCIL
SUPER EXCELLENT MASTER
SELECT MASTER          U.S.A.
ROYAL MASTER          ONLY
TALL CEDARS OF LEBANON
PAST MASTER (VIRTUAL)

FELLOW          CRAFT

ENTERED          APPRENTICE

U.S.A.
ONLY

KNIGHT  COMMANDER
OF THE
COURT OF HONOR

ORDER OF
THE AMARANTH

14

Theatre of the Fraternity

two advanced systems of degrees—either the York Rite or the Ancient and Accepted Scottish Rite. The York Rite provided an additional ten degrees, or moral lessons, and offered the opportunity to don a military uniform and march in displays of solidarity. By contrast, the Scottish Rite consisted of twenty-nine intricate and esoteric degrees that led the candidate on a dramatized historical and religious journey. Unlike the established and powerful York Rite, the Scottish Rite at the turn of the century was a small, dedicated group. By adopting a staged initiation ritual with full theatrical paraphernalia, this fraternal order enjoyed tremendous growth—in terms of both membership and imposing temples—well into the twentieth century.

Scenery created for the Scottish Rite contained exotic images borrowed and adapted from the popular-entertainment stage. Improvements in stage lighting, made possible by the technology of electricity, enhanced this imagery. The resulting material culture enabled the theatre and the fraternity to compete for larger audiences and membership in the more visually oriented early twentieth century. Although most scenery created for the theatre was disposable—meant to be used and replaced with new images to meet the insatiable and changing appetite of the American public—most Scottish Rite scenery, lighting, and stage effects remain intact as installed, locked in a time warp. The fortunate result is that we can glimpse a rich aesthetic heritage that has otherwise been discarded.

The opportunity to appreciate the images and material culture of the fraternities has prompted many questions from both inside and outside the organization. One issue that must be addressed concerns the investigation by "outside" scholars of Scottish Rite initiation practices and stage paraphernalia, which have always been considered secret and proprietary. Thanks to the understanding cooperation of local temples and the sanction of state and national governing bodies, we have been permitted to view fraternal stages and the scenery, costumes, and lighting that were added and adapted to an already established ritual. Significantly, most of the paraphernalia available for study contains little iconography or "secrets" specific to the Scottish Rite.

At the beginning of this project, a Scottish Rite advisory board consisting of recognized Masonic scholars was established to interpret and explain the relative importance of certain proprietary materials. Their participation in the planning symposium helped the contributing academic scholars focus their respective approaches, and the board's consultation on specific information in the essays helped us distinguish between past and present practices of the fraternity. Although the advisory-board members were generous with their vast knowledge of fraternal matters, they never imposed their own interpretation or bias on the contents of the exhibit or catalog.

Several of the essays contain references to the initiation ritual of the Scottish Rite, including Albert Pike's 1857 *The Magnum Opus or Great Work* and Charles T. McClenahan's *The Book of the Ancient and Accepted Scottish Rite of Freemasonry*, first published in 1867. In addition, *The Scotch Rite*

15

*Masonry Illustrated*, an anti-Masonic "exposé" by Jonathan Blanchard, is cited as a source of early ritual practices. Each of these works contains a historical snapshot of initiation practices that occurred in the nineteenth century, but these references in no way depict current ritual, which has been continuously revised, reinterpreted, and modified since these treatises were written.

Much of the discussion in the essays centers around an interpretation of the Scottish Rite based on its successful assimilation of theatrical material culture. Although evidence strongly supports this phenomenon, a missing ingredient should be identified. Conversations with Masons confirm that the presence of costumes, lighting, and scenery attractively enhanced the initiation ritual, but it is also apparent that participation in the Scottish Rite has a profound and deeper meaning that far supersedes these trappings. Most of what we know about these initiation practices is superficial and based on the secondary evidence used to support the essays. After all, only Masons have had the opportunity to experience the individual and collective ethos of the Scottish Rite.

Today, standing in one of the large, elaborately decorated Scottish Rite auditoriums is very much like visiting an old, extant vaudeville theatre or opera house. These spaces have an ephemeral resonance of times gone by. Both environments recall an era when audiences, of both the theatre and the fraternity, sought to escape from their "modern," determinedly progressive world to a distant past that seemed more understandable and orderly. We hope this catalog and exhibit will illuminate and animate this singular period, when the fraternity drew upon the rich artifacts of the theatre to create a profound, provocative initiation experience.

Introduction

KENNETH L. AMES

F I G · 1

A chart by Everett Henry of the various organizations available in Freemasonry. "Busy Brotherly World of Freemasonry: The Ancient Fraternity Is Thriving in America," *Life* 41:15 (Oct. 8, 1956).

THIS COLLECTION OF ESSAYS AND IMAGES INVITES YOU TO EXPLORE THE HEYDAY OF AMERICAN FRATERNAL-ISM, A PERIOD EMBRACING THE FINAL YEARS OF THE NINETEENTH CENTURY AND THE FIRST THIRTY YEARS OF THE TWENTIETH. During these decades, the largest number of voluntary fraternal organizations flourished in America, and lodge membership grew dramatically. Masonic historian S. Brent Morris calculates that in the years between 1885 and 1900 Americans formed more than 150 new fraternal organizations. By 1920, thirty million Americans—half the country's adult population—belonged to one or more of the 800 secret orders then part of American social life. [1]

Within the larger context of fraternal organizations, the once relatively obscure Masonic order of the Scottish Rite stands out with particular clarity—for its explosive growth, for the mass inductions it conducted on an ultimately unprecedented scale, and for the prominent temples it constructed across the nation. According to evidence presented in the following essays, the Scottish Rite's extraordinary rise to prominence was linked in large part to transformations in the nature of its initiation rituals.

The Scottish Rite order of Freemasonry originated in France in the early eighteenth century. Its American roots go back at least as far as 1761, when the Grand Lodge of France and the Council of Emperors authorized Stephen Morin to confer the Rite's twenty-five degrees on this side of the Atlantic. Morin was instrumental in establishing lodges in New York, Philadelphia, Massachusetts, and Charleston, South Carolina, where the Scottish Rite's Supreme Council for the United States was located. Later, a Second Supreme Council was formed in New York, and the Scottish Rite became organized into two jurisdictions: the Northern Jurisdiction in New York, which eventually moved to Boston, and the Southern Jurisdiction, which remained at Charleston.[2]

The Scottish Rite was oriented around a system of incremental or progressive moral education that took the form of a series of ritualized initiations into increasingly higher degrees. In this system, punningly described as "learning by degrees," each successive lesson built upon previous lessons. All lessons, however, revolved around the struggle of "good and evil, insight and ignorance."[3] For much of the nineteenth century, the initiation rituals of the Scottish Rite were personalized if formulaic ceremonies that combined role playing, mysticism, and symbolism. They derived much of their significance from lengthy and sometimes obscure texts that were read aloud. Products of eighteenth-century sensibilities and intellect, these rituals relied heavily on initiates' ability and willingness to attend to the spoken word and to decipher the meanings of symbols and allegories.

Beginning in the 1880s, however, Scottish Rite lodges began to replace this old-style ritual with far more spectacular theatrical performances. These dramatically staged events transformed the nature of the experience for both the initiates and the audience. What had once taken place in the midst of the brothers was now elevated to a stage, thus converting initiates and members into performers and audience, respectively. A ceremony that once integrated the initiate with the membership now conformed to the etiquette, expectations, and visual standards of the commercial theatre. And what had once been largely cerebral if sometimes mystical now became a more multisensory and, above all, more visually oriented experience.

This introduction of a theatrical element into the Masonic lodge heightened the organization's appeal among certain groups of American men and led to a dramatic increase in its membership. With its initiation rituals repackaged as theatrical experiences, the Scottish Rite membership surged throughout the first thirty years of this century. In 1900 about forty thousand men belonged to the Scottish Rite; by 1930 that number had swelled to nearly six hundred thousand.[4] At the same time, the fraternity experienced a frenzy of lodge building. In the largest of these buildings, thousands of men were sometimes simultaneously inducted into the Scottish Rite, a phenomenon that led some to comment on the Rite's "mass production" of members. Around 1930 membership in the Scottish Rite began to drop off, as it did for other fraternal organizations. The Scottish Rite enjoyed a second period of significant growth between 1940 and 1980, when membership again began a gradual decline that continues into the present. Although today the healthiest of this country's fraternal organizations, most of which have declined or disappeared altogether, the Scottish Rite is increasingly a shadow of its former self and may be drifting slowly into extinction.

If a single factor—the transformation of ritual into theatrical performance—accounts for the meteoric rise of the Scottish Rite, the appeal of that factor is more difficult to discern. Why did this new theatricality attract members by the thousands? What does the allure of this novelty indicate about widespread cultural values in this country several decades ago? The messages that emanate from the flowering of the Scottish Rite are many and often contradictory. Some of what we learn from studying the spectacular success of the Scottish Rite illuminates the specific cultural conditions of late-nineteenth- and early-twentieth-century America. But other lessons from this historical episode illuminate issues that transcend mere decades or even centuries.

The most fundamental and significant feature of fraternal organizations is that they are for men only. Beginning with the Odd Fellows' Daughters of Rebekah lodge, created in 1851, many of the major fraternal organizations eventually generated female auxiliaries. These followed the hierarchical structure of male lodges but remained separate and decidedly secondary.[5] The dominant male societies, the Scottish Rite among them, were products of the man-centered world of the eighteenth and nineteenth centuries. Their ideologies and rituals, reflecting prevailing male attitudes and values, were largely devoid of women. Not only were women neither members nor spectators, but they also were neither evoked in ritual nor mentioned in texts. The Masonic realm was created as though women were nonexistent.

In his essay here, William D. Moore reminds us that the Masons' four orders celebrated the male roles of priest, soldier, jester, and craftsman. Significantly, neither father, husband, nor lover was part of this vision. The Masonic world view accepted the "fatherhood of God and the brotherhood of man" while ignoring women and most relationships with them.

Furthermore, some historians of fraternal organizations believe that the explicitly paramilitary character of many societies was a significant part of their appeal, particularly in the decades immediately following the Civil War. Many orders wore regalia similar to military dress, and major meetings and reunions were often marked by spectacular parades of uniformed brothers marching with military precision through city streets. In fact, the same manufacturers who had produced paraphernalia for the military in the 1860s and 1870s prospered in the 1880s by supplying similar material to fraternal organizations.

One way to think about fraternal organizations is as alternative environments, fantasy worlds for men, by men, and about men. The increasingly theatrical quality of the rituals of the

**The path of duty leads to that true light by which we climb the heights of spiritual knowledge and teaches Secrecy, Obedience and Fidelity.**

Scottish Rite drew new members by the thousands precisely because it heightened the affective powers of a fantasy world that had considerable appeal when it was established and that increased over time. Throughout the nineteenth century, the purposes of the ancient Scottish Rite remained much the same, but when the means were aggressively updated, prospective members responded enthusiastically and in great numbers.

Transformations in the rituals of the Scottish Rite occurred against a broader background of gender politics in American society. While opportunities for men expanded in the early years of the nineteenth century, women were increasingly relegated to the domestic sphere. In partial compensation, social arbiters assigned inherent moral superiority to women. Agitation for women's emancipation from stereotyped roles and for suffrage and full participation in American life began before the middle of the century, gradually if not steadily gained strength, and continues today. Meanwhile, the home, the arts, the church, and the theatre were all feminized to varying degrees. [6] By the early twentieth century, many men were reacting to this far-reaching feminization of former male strongholds. The growth of fraternal lodges and the creation of males-only Scottish Rite theatre can be seen as part of that reaction.

The Scottish Rite and other Masonic orders perpetuated a particular vision of manly honor, with roots in the moralistic teaching of the eighteenth century. As Mark Carnes points out, the *exemplum virtutis* ritual associated with each degree illustrated some aspect of manly virtue—particularly reason, the positive uses of aggression, and the value of patriarchy. Masons understood themselves to be a moral elite, although their sense of morality was inculcated within a wholly patriarchal and, therefore, abstracted and fragmented context, generally free from the ambiguities and situational flexibility of women's morality. [7]

The fraternal order was a model society, where the traits of male culture were enshrined and often exaggerated. Hierarchy, a key feature of most patriarchal organizations, was, for example, vital to the Masonic system: Initiates with enough time and money could advance through twenty-nine stages to become thirty-second-degree Masons. The fixed, immutable hierarchy of the Masonic orders offered a security and stability missing in the larger society. Also attractive as a stabilizing agent was the ritual's explicit grounding in the past, exemplified by the prominence of historical figures from King Solomon onward. For many men, the fraternal orders must have represented a world of greater promise and achievement than the one where they spent their working days. At least in the Masons, upward mobility was always possible, downward mobility was unlikely, and truth was unwavering. Here was order in a changing world, in a comfortable and predictable environment free from the challenges and unease generated by women. And perhaps best of all, here were spectacular rituals, staged with glorious costumes, highly affecting settings, and state-of-the-art lighting.

23

No age or society lacks rituals, but during the nineteenth century, protocols and conventions shaped life inside and outside the home in ways that today seem stifling and oppressive.[8] Fraternal societies multiplied during this period, when domestic and social ritual were most elaborate and insistent. The greatest period of Scottish Rite expansion, however, took place as Victorian manners and mores were in decline. This apparent anomaly can be explained in part by recognizing that the Scottish Rite selectively retained or altered its traditional features. For while the core moral and ideational tenets of Freemasonry remained largely intact, there was a significant shift away from an archaic handling of the rituals to a modern method that drew heavily upon advances in current theatrical technology and presentation.

The shift from traditional ritual to new, more theatrical presentations began to take place in new cities, not old, and in the American West, not the East. As it spread rapidly, some members of the society responded negatively. Many others, however, enthusiastically promoted these changes, so successful in attracting new initiates. One factor that probably influenced the decision to transform participatory rituals into viewed spectacles was the increased availability of quality scenery and costumes. Another, more fundamental factor was the growing popularity and widespread acceptance of the theatre in both public and private life. Moralistic restrictions had inhibited American theatre development well into the nineteenth century, but during the second half of the century, theatres became local institutions, and theatrical presentations, both amateur and professional, attracted large, eclectic audiences.

An even more basic reason for the transformation may have been that the Scottish Rite membership recognized how its initiation rituals depended upon a form of melodrama that was becoming increasingly passé. Although the rituals could not easily be changed without overhauling the entire structure of the fraternity, they could be packaged more effectively. In adopting its new theatrical mode, the Scottish Rite decided to put its old wine into new bottles, so to speak. Fortunately for the fraternity, the "new bottles" proved irresistible to many.

The success of this new packaging was tied, in turn, to cultural values and attitudes prevailing in the larger society, particularly to a widespread acceptance of the doctrine of progress. The idea of progress—and the truism that newer was better—had exceptional resonance in the nineteenth century and well into the twentieth. Rising expectations of an improved material life affected virtually all aspects of cultural experience, including Masonic rituals.

At the turn of the century and before, people were inclined to accept the doctrine of progress as a positive force. Great strides in scientific, technological, medical, and educational arenas had transformed the world in ways that would have been almost inconceivable a century before.[9] The major improvements that made America a more comfortable, convenient place to live and work are

FIG·4
A catalog page from the Ihling Bros./Everard
Company shows Worthy Patrons' collars
for use in the women's auxiliary of Eastern Star.
Courtesy of the Livingston Masonic Library,
New York, NY

familiar: steamships, trains, cars, and eventually planes; telephones, radios, and movies; canned foods; central heating; indoor plumbing; and electric lighting and appliances. Americans enjoyed a higher standard of living, as luxuries became necessities and as objects and experiences once accessible only to the upper classes became available to the middle and even the working classes.

Concentrated efforts to increase the speed of production, exploit the economies of scale, and tighten control over the outcome of manufacture revolutionized the quality and availability of consumer goods. The first two factors directly affected price and were driven by competition, at the core of capitalist enterprise. The third enabled manufacturers to more assiduously achieve and maintain a high level of quality, even in such comparatively mundane objects as canning jars, bottles for patent medicine, tools, table flatware, dishes, and glassware. By the 1870s literally thousands of types of objects were being made according to what a previous age would have considered exceptionally high standards. [10] This transformation meant greatly increased profits for manufacturers and an elevated standard of living and heightened expectations for consumers.

What had seemed adequate or even impressive in the past began to appear second-rate and even unacceptable by the late nineteenth and early twentieth centuries. To this more critical mindset, the material and manufactured world of the past now seemed dated and beneath the improved standards of the day. The same assessment could be made of the arts as well. And it may explain why Masons of this era decided to revamp the old-style and no-longer-compelling Scottish Rite rituals.

As Americans became technologically sophisticated, theatres introduced stage sets that were remarkably realistic and powerfully illusionistic. Furthermore, as Lawrence Hill points out, the advent of electrical lighting—arguably the most important theatrical innovation of the period—greatly enhanced the range and subtlety of the dramatic moods that could be evoked. At the same time, rising expectations about the quality of goods and performances throughout the larger society—and particularly among the educated and affluent classes from which the Scottish Rite drew its membership—fostered audiences that were both more demanding and more informed. These two factors—elevated standards of excellence apropos dramatic productions and more sophisticated visual literacy—led to the creation of elaborate stage sets for both commercial theatres and Scottish Rite temples at the turn of the century.

Bringing the Scottish Rite into modern times by theatricalizing its initiation rituals was a savvy marketing decision that recognized the waning appeal of the low-tech, sometimes tedious rituals of the past. The introduction of a theatrical format, complete with professionally painted sets as attractive as those in any theatre, transformed the tired-seeming Masonic rituals into exciting spectacles. The new theatricalized rituals engaged the senses more fully and were much more affecting than their predecessors. Measured in terms of sheer sensory and emotive impact, this was yet another

25

Let the memory of the dead friend cement more firmly the amity of the living, and teaches us
to be zealous and faithful, disinterested and to act as a peacemaker.

instance of progress in American life.

Stage settings for the Scottish Rite and for the commercial theatre were much the same. Both reflected rising standards of excellence, which demanded increased accuracy and awe-inspiring illusions. In both the emphasis was on romantic realism, combining a literal rendering of architecture and natural features with a strong sense of mood. Historical settings, even when imaginary, were based on recognized historical styles. The manner of painting was derived from the dominant academic style of the mid to late nineteenth century, with careful attention to perspective, scale, color, drawing, and the telling detail.[11] The illusionistic power of depicted images contributed significantly to their appeal, while controllable electrical lighting maximized the expressive potential of every set.

The sets designed and built for Scottish Rite temples, painted imitations of three-dimensional reality, provide insight into the imaginary worlds created for a males-only environment. There are few extant stage sets from the late nineteenth and early twentieth centuries because commercial-theatre personnel tended to discard them when a production closed, but Scottish Rite Masons generally retained sets as long as they proved useful backgrounds to the enactment of rituals. Some of these surviving pieces are remarkable works of art, convincingly drawn, floridly colored for dramatic effect, and emotionally charged. Typical Sosman and Landis sets, for example, combine forceful perspective, brilliant color, and attention to textures and details. Unresolved tension between foreground and background elements is a stock design strategy, energizing the scene even before human "actors" make their appearance.

The frequently reproduced scene of the peristyle with "secret words" illustrates this charged foreground-background tension. A neo-grec architectural screen of columns and piers dominates the foreground. (See Carnes, FIG. 17 and Hill, FIGS. 19A,B.) Behind it is a lush Edenic landscape that combines the sublime vision of Thomas Cole's *Voyage of Life* with naturalistic imagery reminiscent of Hawaii or the South Pacific. In the Great Western Stage Company's design for Cyrus's treasury, suggestive detail augments spatial tension. (See Clawson, FIG. 7.) This image displays a rich array of evocative Near Eastern material culture, much of it patterned after illustrated accounts of archaeological excavations, ethnographies, or exhibits at world's fairs.

Stage imagery designed for the Scottish Rite evoked a range of geographical regions and historical epochs. A design for the nineteenth degree, for instance, introduces Gothic imagery. (See Carnes, FIGS. 14, 15.) Contrast this with the scene for the twenty-first degree created by Sosman and Landis that depicts a ruined abbey within a landscape of jagged mountains (FIG. 5). Not only were such scenes realistic, but like most other cultural products, they also had lineage. Scottish Rite members with the most highly developed visual literacy might see these sets both as dramatic settings and

26

F I G · 5

Sosman and Landis created this scenery, used in
the twenty-first degree, for the Scottish Rite
temple in Wichita, Kansas. Courtesy of the Scottish
Rite Bodies of Wichita, KS

F I G · 6

(below) A page from the M.C. Lilley Company catalog
shows marshal parade sashes for members of
the Grand United Order of Odd Fellows. Courtesy
of the Livingston Masonic Library, New York, NY

as derivative cultural artifacts rich in references to previous imagery. Recognizing those antecedents was part of the pleasure of viewing the sets.

Changes in the media of the rituals—that is, the addition of elaborate stage sets, ornate costumes, and the expressive range of lighting made possible by electrification—also changed the relationship between the performances or presentations and those who participated in them. As the rituals became dramatic spectacles, the role of the initiates shifted in notable ways. The single initiate was increasingly replaced by multiple initiates, all of whom were more or less passive. Fraternity members also became passive spectators or, sometimes, actors or even stagehands. To some critics, these mass initiations of scores or more seemed the most disturbing lapse from past practice, suggesting the increasing superficiality of Freemasonry. They worried that gaudy spectacle was taking the place of a somber commitment to a community dedicated to timeless virtue.

Part of what makes the theatricalization of Scottish Rite initiation rituals so fascinating is the convergence of two very different sets of cultural values. On the one hand was a system of moral education formulated in the eighteenth century and based on eighteenth-century cultural conditions and technology. On the other were theatre sets and technology representative of modern capitalist thinking. The radical changes in Freemasonry in the early years of this century reflected the impact of the market mentality and quantitative thinking, the addiction to bigness, and the predominance of the profit motive. The great transformation of the Scottish Rite was yet another example of the ubiquitous market principle at work: The fraternity emphasized the most marketable aspect of its activity, and its dues-paying membership soared. The income produced by those increases made it possible, in turn, to create larger and more lavish buildings and to stage even more spectacular initiation rituals. As growth became the major goal of the organization or, at least, its major outward manifestation, initiate involvement in the ritual became increasingly depersonalized and remote. Appearance overtook substance. Expansion rather than moral indoctrination became the driving force behind the order.

Although the world in which the Scottish Rite flourished has changed significantly, relics of that Masonic order remain in the form of majestic temples still used by some memberships. Today, however, comparatively few people even enter a Masonic temple, once the site of ancient rites performed in lavish costumes before sets that rivaled those used in vaudeville and the legitimate theatre. Even if many of the attractions of Freemasonry seem elusive to us at the end of the twentieth century, the surviving artifacts of this venerable fraternity generate an undeniable

27

7TH DEGREE • PROVOST AND JUDGE

Teaches us to decide justly and impartially and to do justice to all men.

8TH DEGREE • INTENDANT OF THE BUILDING

Ever remember he is your brother, and teaches us that we should be Charitable,
Benevolent and Sympathetic, recognizing the dignity of labor.

sense of awe, mystery, and admiration.

This catalog and the exhibition it accompanies make it possible to once again sense the magic and power of these environments and the sets that enhanced them. These objects offer us a glimpse of an earlier America, one poised precariously between the moral idealism of the nineteenth century and the appearance-oriented culture of the twentieth. These captivating images tentatively fuse both cultural systems, simultaneously looking backward and forward. When they were painted, their creators imbued these sets with a spatial tension that heightened their dramatic impact. Today, in retrospect, we recognize that they also embody cultural tensions. Together these two layers of tension, visual and cultural, add intrigue to already fascinating creations.

FIG · 7

The earliest fraternal costumes were decorative robes used to conceal everyday dress.

Courtesy of the Museum of Our National Heritage, Lexington, MA

Theatre of the Fraternity

$^1$ S. Brent Morris, "Boom to Bust in the Twentieth Century: Freemasonry and American Fraternities," the 1988 Anson Jones Lecture, presented to the Texas Lodge of Research, March 19, 1989.

$^2$ A concise history of the Scottish Rite and a glossary of Masonic terms appear in a reunion program, *Towards the Light*, Guthrie, OK, n.d.

$^3$ *Towards the Light*, 14.

$^4$ Morris, "Boom to Bust," 8–9.

$^5$ For an account of women's activities in support of Freemasonry, see William D. Moore, "Funding the Temples of Masculinity: Women's Roles in Masonic Fairs in New York State, 1870–1930," *Nineteenth Century* 14, no.1 (1994), 19–25.

$^6$ On increasing feminization, see Ann Douglas, *The Feminization of American Culture* (New York: Knopf, 1977), and Sandra Sizer, *Gospel Hymns and Social Religion* (Philadelphia: Temple University Press, 1979).

$^7$ Male and female moral and ethical systems are compared in Carol Gilligan, *In a Different Voice* (Cambridge: Harvard University Press, 1982).

$^8$ On the ritualization of Victorian life, see Kenneth L. Ames, *Death in the Dining Room and Other Tales of Victorian Culture* (Philadelphia: Temple University Press, 1992), 7–43, and John Kasson, *Rudeness and Civility: Manners in Nineteenth-Century America* (New York: Hill and Wang, 1990).

$^9$ On progress, especially technological, see Siegfried Giedion, *Mechanization Takes Command* (New York: Norton, 1969), and David A. Hanks *et al.*, *Innovative Furniture in America* (New York: Horizon, 1981). For an assessment of American cultural values of the late nineteenth century, see Howard Mumford Jones, *The Age of Energy: Varieties of American Experience, 1865–1915* (New York: Viking, 1970).

$^{10}$ On the proliferation of quality-controlled manufactures, see Deborah Federhan *et al.*, *Accumulation and Display: Mass Marketing Household Goods in America, 1880–1920* (Winterthur: Winterthur Museum, 1986).

$^{11}$ For parallels in American history painting, see William Ayres, ed., *Picturing History: American Painting, 1770–1930* (New York: Rizzoli, 1993).

FIG · 1

Composite room, Masonic temple, New
York City, Napoleon LeBrun, architect, ca. 1875.
Courtesy of the Livingston Masonic Library,
New York, NY

# SCOTTISH RITE

## WILLIAM D. MOORE

FREEMASONRY WAS MOST POPULAR AND INFLUENTIAL IN THE UNITED STATES IN THE DECADES SURROUNDING THE TURN OF THE TWENTIETH CENTURY, WHEN AMERICAN MEN JOINED FOUR INTERRELATED, BUT ORGANIZATIONALLY SEPARATE, MASONIC GROUPS. These bodies—"craft," "Blue Lodge," or "symbolic" Masonry; the Scottish Rite; the York Rite; and the Ancient Arabic Order of Nobles of the Mystic Shrine, better known as the Shriners—performed distinct initiation rites but shared overlapping memberships. If he desired, a man could participate in all four organizations.

The first three degrees of Freemasonry, which together constituted the historical and structural prototype of the other three groups, had been formalized in the eighteenth century. Variously called "craft," "symbolic," and "Blue Lodge" Masonry, its membership met in local Masonic lodges. The remaining three organizations assumed their modern form in the nineteenth century and required participants to hold active membership in a Masonic lodge.

The groups all ritually imparted symbolic identities to their participants. Upon joining a Masonic lodge, for example, a man metaphorically became a worker in stone. After undergoing all the rituals of the York Rite, he was a Knight Templar, a successor to the crusading Christian soldiers of the Middle Ages. Membership in the Shrine transformed a participant into an Arab noble, and a gentleman initiated into the Scottish Rite could consider himself an adept schooled in the secret wisdom of the ages.

All four Masonic bodies needed spaces in which to enact their rituals and other activities. The Blue Lodges met in lodge rooms within buildings called Masonic temples or halls (FIG. 1). The Knights Templar met in spaces they called asylums and practiced martial precision marching in drill halls (FIG. 2). The Shriners built elaborate neo-Islamic mosques to house their raucous burlesque ceremonials (FIG. 3), and the Scottish Rite enacted their initiations in spaces identified as cathedrals [1] (FIG. 4). The twenty-nine Scottish Rite rituals were far more complex than those of the other Masonic bodies, drawing upon biblical narratives, Neoplatonic symbolism, Rosicrucianism, cabalistic numerology, alchemy, Hermetic thought, and other mystical traditions. Participants in these initiation ceremonies were introduced to most of the important strains of Western esoteric thought.

Although the Scottish Rite's philosophy and teachings varied only slightly during the period between 1870 and 1930, its membership increased exponentially, and its ritual performance practices changed radically. [2] In the 1860s, one candidate was initiated at a time in largely verbal ceremonies enacted privately in small gatherings. By the 1920s, thousands of men were inducted simultaneously into the organization by passively observing visual spectacles presented in massive, elaborate theatrical spaces.

The transformation in the organization's ceremonial life occurred in a dialectical rela-

FIG · 2
Asylum of California Commandery No. 1, San
Francisco, 1896. Courtesy of the Livingston Masonic
Library, New York, NY

FIG · 3
Irem Temple Mosque, Wilkes-Barre,
Pennsylvania, Olds & Puckey, architects, 1909.
Courtesy of the author

Theatre of the Fraternity

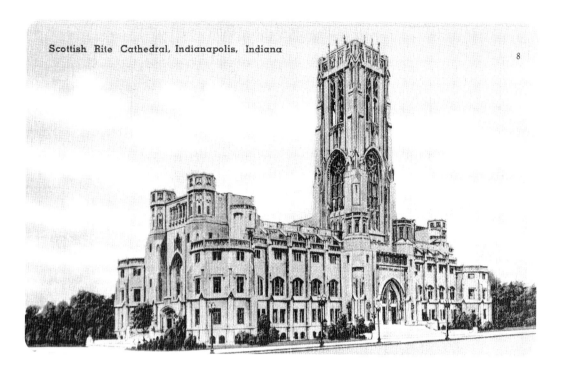

Scottish Rite Cathedral, Indianapolis, Indiana

8

**FIG · 4**
Scottish Rite cathedral, Indianapolis, Indiana,
George F. Schreiber, architect, 1929. Courtesy of
the Livingston Masonic Library, New York, NY

tionship with the objects and structures the membership used to enact its rites.[3] New ritual practices and patterns of material culture developed simultaneously. The innovative objects and buildings produced to enhance the fraternity's initiation rites altered the ways participants behaved and understood the experience of belonging to the Scottish Rite.

During this period of growth and transformation, Scottish Rite members in the United States spent millions of dollars on edifices and paraphernalia to support the ceremony of initiation. Ritual objects ranged from the ephemeral to the monumental and included items from inexpensive disposable props to buildings that cost fortunes to erect. An analysis of the extensive and varied material culture of the Rite during this period provides insights that are inaccessible in the written record, and the spaces where Scottish Rite rituals were enacted are a particularly fertile field for tracing the group's growth and flux. By transforming its ritual spaces, the Scottish Rite radically reshaped itself during the period under investigation. Furthermore, a consideration of these spaces within the larger context of Masonic architecture indicates that Scottish Rite cathedrals played an integral role in constructing a complex multifaceted Masonic identity for American men at the turn of the century.

### Masonic Lodge Rooms

A discussion of the spaces of the Scottish Rite necessarily begins with a description of the lodge room where the first three degrees of Freemasonry, the "symbolic" or "Blue Lodge" degrees, were enacted.[4] By the mid-nineteenth century, the Masonic lodge room had acquired a ritually determined form. This architectural space, represented in an illustration from Duncan's *Ritual* (FIG. 5), a guide to the Masonic ritual from the second half of the nineteenth century, was constructed with little variation wherever a Masonic lodge met in the United States and continues to be reproduced in the meeting rooms of the fraternity to this day.[5]

The rectangular lodge room was located above street level, with entrances arranged symmetrically on one of the short sides. A chair for the Master of the lodge was located centrally

33

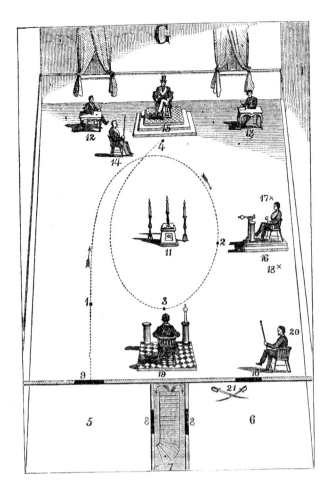

FIG·7
(opposite) Egyptian lodge room, Masonic temple,
Colorado Springs, Colorado, ca. 1900. Courtesy of
the Livingston Masonic Library, New York, NY

FIG·5
Lodge-room diagram from Duncan's *Ritual*.
Courtesy of the Livingston Masonic Library,
New York, NY

FIG·6
An 1855 chromolithograph of the grand lodge
room of the Masonic temple in Philadelphia.
Courtesy of the Museum of Our National Heritage,
Lexington, MA — Photography: John Miller
Documents

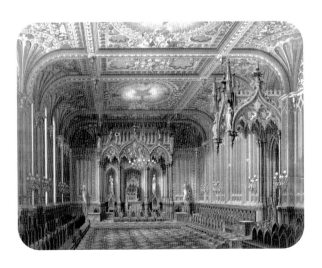

Theatre of the Fraternity

against the wall facing the doors, and a similar chair for the lodge's Senior Warden was positioned opposite the Master's chair along the wall between the doors. A third officer's chair, that of the Junior Warden, was placed against the center of the long wall on the Master's left side. For ritual purposes, the Master and his chair were understood to reside in the east, while the Senior Warden occupied the west and the Junior Warden, the south. A pair of imaginary axes, terminating in the primary officers' chairs, ran east-west and north-south, thus ordering the space within the room.

Other officers of the lodge, including the secretary and treasurer, were situated ritually, but most of the lodge's membership occupied unassigned seating arranged around the room's walls. An altar occupied the center of the room, where the axes crossed, and was surrounded by empty floor space. The composite room of Napoleon LeBrun's Masonic temple, built in New York City between 1870 and 1875, is typical of the hundreds of thousands of Masonic lodge rooms constructed in the United States at the end of the nineteenth and beginning of the twentieth centuries (FIGS. 1, 12).

The lodge room was designed to serve several specific functions. Most importantly, it was an alternative realm set apart from day-to-day reality, and many of its features enhanced this otherworldly quality. For example, windows, when present, were shuttered or positioned high on the edifice to remove the distractions of the street and to prevent eavesdropping.[6] A set of stairs isolated the space from the pedestrian realm, while the Tyler, an officer with a sword, ensured that only members were admitted to the room during meetings. Soundproofing often further buffered the ritual space from the outside world. Revivalist ornamentation, like the Gothic details in Philadelphia's grand lodge room and the Egyptian motifs found in the Colorado Springs Masonic temple of about 1905, artificially separated the room from the time period in which it existed (FIGS. 6, 7). Historical motifs on the walls and furniture of the rooms allowed members to immerse themselves in a milieu removed from the temporal reality of their daily lives and the commonplace details of their personal identities. A primary purpose of this isolated space was to facilitate the membership's identification with the unbroken chain of brothers that, according to Masonic ritual and literature, stretched backward to eternity.

The lodge-room floor plan also expressed concepts of hierarchy, egalitarianism, and group cohesion. The elaborately ornamented chairs that the lodge officers occupied were often monumental in scale and were elevated above the floor by a ritually prescribed number of steps.[7] The design and positioning of this furniture conferred an exalted status upon the individuals chosen to occupy it.

While the status of the lodge officers was enhanced by the furniture associated with their position, the chairs arrayed around the walls of the room for the general membership were the material manifestation of the fraternity's ideology of egalitarianism. All members not serving as

35

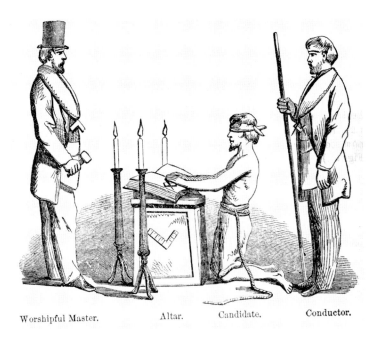

FIG · 8

Candidate taking the oath of a Master Mason, from Duncan's *Ritual*. Courtesy of the Livingston Masonic Library, New York, NY

Worshipful Master.     Altar.     Candidate.     Conductor.

officers occupied interchangeable seats of identical status. Facing the center of the room, this furniture also reinforced the institutional identity of the lodge. While meeting in a lodge room, Freemasons observed their peers, their brothers, face to face. Unlike a commercial theatre or traditional Christian church, where the seating is arranged so the audience sees the faces of the individuals in front and the backs of the heads of most others in attendance, the lodge room fostered a sense of community by supporting interpersonal observations. By facing the center and encircling the room, lodge-room seating ensured that each individual both saw and was seen by everyone present. This mutual observation provided the membership with a concrete image for the abstract concept of a brotherhood, reinforced the corporate identity of the fraternity, and tightened the "mystic tie" that supposedly bound them. In some of the largest lodge rooms, a balcony increased the seating capacity, but these structures affected neither the function nor the ideological significance of the room. [8]

The focus of the entire room was the altar, which occupied the center where the two axes intersected. All seats faced this point, sanctified by a Bible and highlighted by ceremonially lit candles known as the "lesser lights" (FIG. 8). At the altar, the candidate crossed the thresholds of the Masonic rites of passage: Here the "profane" was "brought to light," as a man was transformed into a Freemason before the assembled brotherhood.

The open space surrounding the altar set it apart symbolically from the furnishings of the room and served a practical ceremonial function. The dramatic action of the Masonic ritual occurred in this space. The central narrative of Freemasonry, the story of the murder of Hiram Abiff, the overseer of the building of Solomon's temple, was ritually enacted, with the initiate taking the primary role and the lodge brethren functioning as the supporting cast (FIG. 9). The dramatic actions of the initiation ceremony, called "floorwork" by members of the fraternity, included the symbolic death, burial, and exhumation of the candidate.

During the floorwork of the Masonic ritual, lodge members portrayed individuals drawn from the biblical account of the building of Solomon's temple. The Master of the lodge became King Solomon, and the Senior Deacon played the role of Hiram, the king of Tyre, who supplied Solomon with materials to build his great temple. During the enactment of the ritual, the lodge room symbolically represented Solomon's temple and was identified as such by a pair of pillars at the west end of all such rooms. As seen in the Colorado Springs lodge room, these pillars represent those that, according to the Bible, Solomon erected on the porch of his temple (FIG. 7).

Because of the Masonic belief that Freemasonry had been practiced throughout the history of Western civilization, revivalist decor reinforced the primary symbolic identity of the lodge room and prompted further associations and identities. The Gothic design scheme of the Philadelphia grand lodge room exemplifies this layering of Masonic architectural meaning. Nineteenth-century

F I G · 9

The murder of Hiram Abiff, "floorwork" of the
third degree. From Jabez Richardson, *Richardson's
Monitor of Free-Masonry* (New York: Dick &
Fitzgerald, 1860). Courtesy of the Livingston
Masonic Library, New York, NY

F I G · 10

Ritual room for the degree of the Knights Elect of
Nine, from Charles T. McClenachan, *The Book
of the Ancient and Accepted Scottish Rite of
Freemasonry* (New York: Masonic Publishing and
Manufacturing Co., 1867). Courtesy of the
Livingston Masonic Library, New York, NY

F I G · 11

Diagram of the ritual room of the Knights
Elect of Nine, from *The Secret Directory,* undated.
Courtesy of the Livingston Masonic Library,
New York, NY

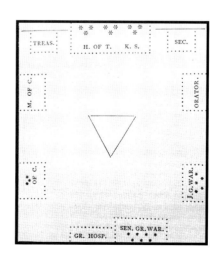

37

Masonic belief systems argued that Freemasonry, also known as "the Craft," had been practiced in the Middle Ages by both the crusading Knights Templar and the workmen who built the great cathedrals of Europe.[9] In this romantic vision, the "ancient brethren" of the medieval period had assumed the roles of Solomon, Hiram Abiff, and Hiram, king of Tyre, in enacting the rites. By performing the supposedly unchanging Masonic ritual in a lodge room designed to mimic a medieval interior, the Masons of late-nineteenth-century Pennsylvania were identifying themselves simultaneously with cathedral builders, crusading knights, and ancient biblical patriarchs. Similarly, in the early twentieth century, lodge rooms decorated in a Colonial Revival style allowed members of the fraternity to occupy the roles of both Colonial American Freemasons and Solomon and his associates. Beginning in the 1870s, Masonic temples in cities such as Chicago, Philadelphia, and New York contained several lodge rooms decorated in a range of architectural styles. Members meeting in these series of rooms on different nights were reminded of the many layers of Masonic history. Solomon's temple, however, remained the primary symbolic identity of the space, regardless of the design aesthetic.

### *Scottish Rite Lodge Rooms*

When Scottish Rite membership began to grow following the Civil War, the organization's prescriptive literature called for ceremonies to be held in spaces similar to those used for the rituals of the first three Masonic degrees. In 1867 Charles T. McClenachan published a guide to the Scottish Rite that included instructions for all the degrees practiced by the Rite in America.[10] In this volume, an illustration of the ritual room for the ninth degree, known as the Knights Elect of Nine, shows a space similar in form to those used in the first three Masonic degrees (FIG. 10). The rectangular space is longer than it is wide and is bisected longitudinally by an axis originating with an officer seated in a centrally located, elevated position against the far wall. Seats line the side walls, and an altar appears near the center of the open floor. A diagram from another contemporary guide to the Scottish Rite ritual also illustrates a space similar to that used in the Blue Lodge degrees (FIG. 11).[11] The open floor around the altar again provides the space necessary for the floorwork integral to the ritual. New York City's 1870 Masonic temple included a room on the fifth floor, called the council chamber, designed to meet the spatial needs of the city's Scottish Rite bodies (FIG. 12).

Because Scottish Rite rituals were written to be performed by Masons who had completed the first three degrees, an understandable similarity exists between the prescribed Scottish Rite ritual space of post–Civil War America and the standard Masonic lodge room. The rituals of these "higher degrees" drew upon a ceremonial vocabulary based upon the Blue Lodge degrees and familiar to the Masonic member-

10TH DEGREE • ELU OF THE FIFTEEN

38

FIG · 12

(opposite) Council chamber, Masonic temple, New
York City, Napoleon LeBrun, architect, ca.
1875. Courtesy of the Livingston Masonic Library,
New York, NY

FIG · 13

Scottish Rite hall, Masonic temple, Montgomery
and Post Streets, San Francisco, 1896. Courtesy of
the Livingston Masonic Library, New York, NY

ship. In addition to utilizing a similar space, each degree, for example, had its own distinct apron, pass-
word, handshake, and set of gestures of recognition. [12]

Because of the narrative and philosophical scope of the Scottish Rite degrees, the
required ritual chambers differed from the spaces of the first three degrees in the complexity of their
prescribed ornamentations. McClenachan's descriptions of the ritual chambers in which the fourth
through thirty-second degrees were performed become increasingly elaborate. Draperies of various
colors and patterns were required, as were columns, candlesticks, altars of many shapes, and thrones
of differing designs. While the lodge room represented Solomon's temple in the first three degrees, the
Scottish Rite membership used ceremonial props and furnishings to transform the ritual space into
various romantic locations, including a cavern, a secret vault beneath Solomon's temple, a bridge, the
throne room of a Persian king, the road to Jerusalem, the summit of a mountain, a military encampment in the desert, and the court of Saladin. [13]

FIG · 14

East end of the preceptory of Oriental consistory, Masonic temple, Chicago, 1893. Courtesy of the Livingston Masonic Library, New York, NY

When the Scottish Rite degrees were first enacted in most American cities, they were presented in rooms housing other Masonic groups. [14] The Scottish Rite organizations outfitted these lodge rooms with the paraphernalia required for the higher degrees, often improvising and manufacturing materials themselves. [15] In 1883, for example, John J. Stewart, a member of the El Paso, Texas, Lodge of Perfection No. 5, manufactured a set of Scottish Rite furnishings under the personal supervision of Albert Pike, the Sovereign Grand Commander of the Scottish Rite in the Southern Jurisdiction. [16] The fraternal regalia firms that came to prominence following the Civil War also manufactured a range of materials to support the enactment of the higher-degree rituals. [17] As Scottish Rite bodies prospered, they accumulated such extensive holdings of regalia that their chambers acquired an identity distinct from those used in conferring the first three degrees. A 1896 photograph of the Scottish Rite hall of San Francisco's Masonic temple at Montgomery and Post Streets reveals the variety of equipment used within the degrees (FIG. 13). While this room retains some characteristics of a standard Masonic lodge room—most notably a centrally located altar and elevated, ornamented ceremonial chairs—other details, such as the banister demarcating one end of the room, indicate that the space no longer represents only Solomon's temple.

### The Introduction of Scenery

The story line of the first three degrees of Freemasonry was a relatively simple tale that occurred in one location, in one time period, and with one set of characters. [18] By contrast, the Scottish Rite rituals attempted to school initiates in varying esoteric traditions by incorporating characters from throughout Europe and the Middle East and by focusing on events that spanned millennia. To accept an enclosed room in an American city as Solomon's temple required a leap of faith and imagination. To picture that same room as, interchangeably and sequentially, the throne room of a Persian king, a mountain top, and a military encampment demanded a more developed romantic vision.

To facilitate the suspension of disbelief required by the rituals, theatrical lighting and scenery were introduced into the performance of the Scottish Rite degrees in the early 1890s. The use of painted scenery both expedited the job of preparing the ritual space and resulted in more convincing settings. Members no longer needed to hang elaborate draperies and move quantities of furniture; instead, by pulling ropes and changing drops they easily could transform rustic caves into royal Persian palaces. Further, the use of lighting equipment made it possible to represent mystical visions, miracles, and the passing of time. By varying light and color intensity, stagehands could transform morning into midday and subsequently into evening and night, all within a few minutes or hours.

At first, painted scenery simply was incorporated into the east end of an otherwise standard Scottish Rite lodge room, as is evident in the preceptory of Oriental consistory on the eighteenth floor of the Masonic temple in Chicago (FIG. 14). This space, with seating on three sides and an altar in the center surrounded by open space for floorwork, was revolutionary only in that it included scenery in the room's east end. [19] The backdrop functioned as the eastern wall of the room, terminating the elevated platform where the officers' chairs traditionally were located (FIGS. 1, 13). In explaining the use of scenery for the Scottish Rite degrees, Charles E. Rosenbaum, a leading innovator within the fraternity, wrote, "It must be understood that a Scottish Rite stage is not to be conceived of as a theatrical stage, for when so considered much of its effective use is destroyed, but when used as a combination with the floor of the auditorium, giving to the initiate a beautiful picture for the eye, while at the same time he is lending an attentive ear to the lessons that are being taught, the use of such a stage will be understood and correspondingly valued." [20]

Members of the Scottish Rite in Yankton, South Dakota, installed scenic material in their cathedral in 1906. Again, the scenery was an evolutionary development of the Masonic lodge room rather than a revolutionary departure from the standard space. In describing Yankton's use of scenery in the *New Age*, the official organ of the Southern Jurisdiction of the Scottish Rite, Robert E. McDowell explained, "It is not the purpose, of course, to have a complete theatrical equipment but only such as would be suitable and necessary for the proper and effective display in connection with the work upon the floor of the auditorium, thus bringing in apt illustration before the eye as well as to the ear of a candidate the lessons and teachings of the various degrees." [21] In Yankton, as in the consistory room in Chicago, the stage and its drops provided a scenic context, while the action of the ritual, the floorwork, occurred in the space around the altar at the center of the room. The seats continued to be located in the traditional arrangement for a lodge room, primarily along the north and south walls. At thirty-six feet wide by fifty feet long, the space still could be considered intimate. [22]

The incorporation of theatrical technology into the Scottish Rite ritual—including scenery, costumes, lights, and public-address systems—meant the fraternity could initiate simultaneously large numbers of candidates. Local organizations no longer had to focus their efforts on a single initiate for the experience to be effective. The use of scenic visual aids enabled scores of individuals to be impressed by the grandeur of the rituals. Instead of each new member participating in the degrees, one individual, the *exemplar*, physically experienced the ritual while a group of candidates observed.

The introduction of exemplars and theatrical techniques had economic ramifications. The more new members that a local organization passed through the degrees, the greater the sum of initiation fees collected. As a group's treasury increased, it could afford a larger facility and could bring in even more members. [23] The resulting dynamic produced increasingly grand buildings, with more and more elaborate scenery and paraphernalia and ever larger ritual spaces. When Scottish Rite organizations first sought spaces for their exclusive use, they often purchased structures originally erected

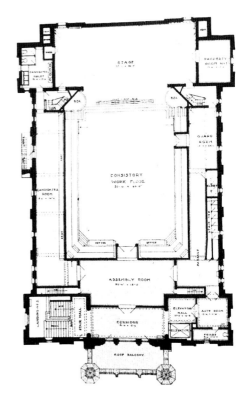

**FIG · 15**
Floor plans of the Scottish Rite cathedral, Fort Wayne, Indiana, Mahurin & Mahurin, architects, ca. 1915. Courtesy of the Livingston Masonic Library, New York, NY

**FIG · 16**
Interior of the Scottish Rite cathedral, Fort Wayne, Indiana, Mahurin & Mahurin, architects, ca. 1915. Courtesy of the Livingston Masonic Library, New York, NY

Theatre of the Fraternity

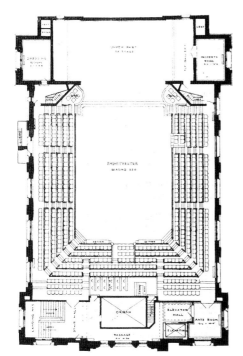

Wisdom is the true Masonic Light. It teaches us that through the Beneficence of God we have within us the capacity to obtain Wisdom and Power and become Leaders of men.

as churches; for example, in 1899 the St. Louis Scottish Rite bodies purchased the former Second Presbyterian Church, located on the northwest corner of Seventeenth and Locust Streets.[24] Frequently, these buildings were sold after the organizations built larger and grander edifices.

### Enlarged Lodge Rooms and Theatres

While the Supreme Councils of the Scottish Rite, located in Boston and the District of Columbia at the turn of the century, acted as the fraternity's governing bodies, they allowed local organizations to retain control over the design, financing, and construction of buildings.[25] Decentralized authority, combined with ongoing innovation in ritual practices, resulted in variation in the design of hundreds of these ritual spaces built across the country. In every temple erected, the architect and the building committee reached a unique solution to the problem of providing a space that allowed scenery to be used in conferring the degrees upon large classes of men. All these solutions combined elements of two architectural models: the lodge room and the theatre. Each space existed somewhere on a continuum connecting these two paradigms.

The Fort Wayne, Indiana, Scottish Rite cathedral, designed by the firm of Mahurin & Mahurin, for example, features a central lodge room so large that an anonymous commentator in a Masonic periodical described it as "taking advantage of the historical efficiency of the Stadium" (FIGS. 15, 16). According to this writer, the seats, accommodating up to 550 spectators and installed on steep risers, "form three sides of the 'stadium,' the stage being the fourth." In the plans for this building, the stadium's center is identified as the "consistory work floor." Although it features footlights, the stage is distinguished from the floor by only three steps. Visiting dignitaries were honored by being placed, in their traditional Masonic positions, against the east wall in elevated boxes on the northeast and southeast corners of the stage. These seats, like those on the side walls of the cathedral, faced the cen-

43

FIG · 18
Scottish Rite cathedral, Masonic temple, Detroit,
George D. Mason & Co., architects, completed
1926. Courtesy of the Livingston Masonic Library,
New York, NY

FIG · 19
(below) Floor plan of the Scottish Rite cathedral,
Detroit, George D. Mason & Co., architects,
published 1922. Courtesy of the Avery
Architectural and Fine Arts Library, Columbia
University in the City of New York

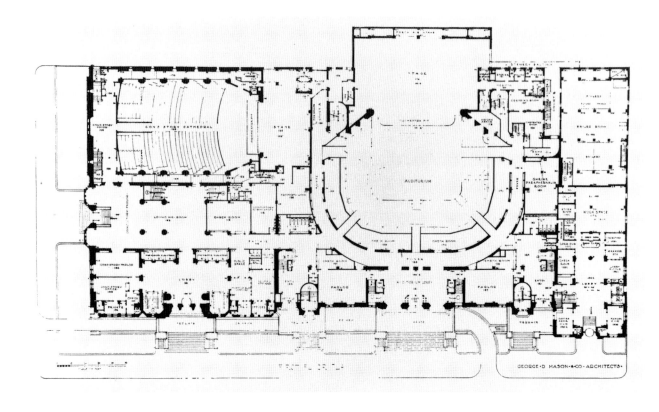

Theatre of the Fraternity

FIG·20
Scottish Rite cathedral, St. Louis, William B. Ittner,
architect, 1924. Courtesy of the Missouri Historical
Society, St. Louis, MO

ter of the room rather than the stage.[26]

The ritual space of the Scottish Rite cathedral constructed in Los Angeles between 1905 and 1906 falls midway on the continuum between expanded lodge rooms and the more purely theatrical auditoriums. Hailed as "the most ornate and complete structure utilized by any body of Scottish Rite Masons in America, and probably in the world," the Los Angeles cathedral was constructed of steel, brick, terra cotta, and marble on a lot 120 feet wide by 155 feet deep.[27] The auditorium, described as the "glory of the Cathedral," was twice as large as the ritual space in Yankton, measuring 65 by 106 feet, with a stage measuring 62 by 32 feet.[28] The standard three low steps separated the floor of the auditorium from the stage, but seats no longer lined the room's long side walls. Rather, the 1,100 chairs for the audience, arrayed against the west wall, were aligned opposite the stage, eighty-four scenic drops, and the proscenium arch, which defined the short wall at the end of the room's long axis. While the ritual action of the degree still took place upon the floor of the ritual space, the new configuration of the seating in this cathedral transformed the experience for the audience. Occupying 375 seats located in an overhanging balcony, the candidates now were situated so they observed the ritual action but did not see their peers (FIG. 17); the architecture had changed their role from that of participant to isolated, passive observer.

The Scottish Rite cathedral in Detroit's spectacular Masonic temple, designed by George D. Mason and dedicated in 1926, represents the theatrical end of the spectrum (FIGS. 18, 19). In this auditorium, described when it was new as "a modern theater, capable of seating nearly seventeen hundred persons," performance space is demarcated from the audience.[29] The stage is located several feet above the chairs in the front row. All seats, even those in the dignitaries' boxes, face the proscenium arch, so audience members see only their peers' backs. The stage has taken the place of the auditorium floor as the site of the ritual floorwork.[30]

The Scottish Rite cathedral of St. Louis, Missouri, completed in 1924 for more than $2 million, represents another possible configuration for ritual space. The auditorium of this fantastic building, designed by William B. Ittner to seat 2,950 people, features a ninety-eight-foot proscenium arch that dominates the space (FIG. 20). The axes in this auditorium have shifted away from those of the traditional lodge room. The east end of the room, signified by the stage, no longer defines the end of the space's primary axis; rather, the spatial emphasis has changed, and the long axis now runs par-

45

Be not deceived! God has formed thy nature. His Law can never be abrogated, nor His Justice eluded and forever and ever it will be true that "whatsoever a man soweth, that shall he also reap."

allel to both the stage and the audience, seated in fixed chairs on steeply pitched risers. This transformation, with the broadened stage and reduced distance between the individual and the scenery, means the observer's field of vision is filled, so the observer experiences minimal visual distractions. Ironically, the vast dimensions that created this sense of individual isolation also meant that the auditorium could accommodate monumental groups of initiates. In fact, this cathedral's inaugural class, held in May 1924, included 1,000 candidates. [51] (See Clawson, FIGS. 15, 16.)

The introduction of theatrical technology not only transformed the architectural space where the rituals were performed, but it also changed how initiates experienced receiving the degrees of the Scottish Rite. Although innovations in ritual presentation were largely accepted, a few conservative voices decried what they perceived as a degradation of the fraternity's practices. "The tendency of the time," a commentator wrote in 1906, "is to relegate the onlookers (the Brethren) to mere spectators of a theatrical performance. They are perched up in a gallery and have no more to do with the ceremonies of the evening than a man who buys a seat in the dress circle of a theatre at a grand spectacular show. There is a coldness about this that strikes me as most un-masonic." [52]

Ten years later H. R. Evans, a thirty-third-degree Mason from Washington, D.C., made a similar point when he wrote, "The tendency has been to make a theatre of the Scottish Rite Cathedral . . . I have always felt that I was not in a Masonic Temple but in a theatre; that I was not a part of the affair but a mere spectator. In a Blue Lodge I never had this feeling, because there was no stage, everything was done on the floor; I was an actual participant in the degree . . . I prefer floor work; the more the better." [53]

At the heart of the traditionalists' concerns about floorwork, spectatorship, and "coldness" was an appreciation for the degrees' lessons. Francis H. E. O'Donnell voiced these apprehensions most eloquently in a screed titled "Philosophy and the Drama in Freemasonry," published in the *New Age* in 1906. In this inflammatory piece, O'Donnell claims the fraternity is being cheapened by theatrical presentations and that new members are leaving their initiations with imperfect understandings of the fraternity's teachings. In his opinion, the visual aids Rosenbaum heralded were interfering with the verbal truths at the basis of Freemasonry's teachings. He continued:

If Masonic work is to degenerate into miserable dramatic misrepresentations of Divine Truths enacted by self-conscious imitators of histrionic art, then away with such trumpery. The attentive ear can listen, and learn, always, everywhere, to the instructive tongue. The glory of the Celestial Being is as interesting and recognizable to the anxious, eager seeker after Truth, when communicated in the darkest recesses of a mountain cave, as when surrounded by all the scenic effects and pictures of the finest Scottish Rite Cathedral . . . Elegantly prepared tableaux and scenic effects may serve to impress striking truths upon minds of coars-

F I G · 2 1
Scottish Rite cathedral, Meridian, Mississippi, Penn
J. Krouse, architect, 1914; burned ca. 1985.
Courtesy of the Livingston Masonic Library, New
York, NY

er fibre, but the TRUTH itself—burned in by the inspired words of the faithful teacher—is what will ever most appeal to the finer mentality of the earnest seeker for the LIGHT. [34]

### Scottish Rite Cathedral Designs

Building committees that determined the floor plans of their structures also chose an architectural style for both the interior and exterior. The rich tradition of revivalist ornamentation evident in Masonic building practices was reaffirmed in the design of Scottish Rite cathedrals. Although discussion occurred concerning which revivalist style should be employed for cathedrals, in all cases the arguments were based upon a conception of the Rite as a conduit for the transmission of ancient mysteries passed down by initiates over the ages. This secret knowledge supposedly had descended to the present from ancient Egypt, through the biblical patriarchs, the Greek philosophers, the cathedral builders, and the Knights Templar. [35] Because of this presumed pedigree for the Scottish Rite, advocates argued for Egyptian, Gothic, and classical ornamentation for cathedrals. "The apartments where the degrees are given," H. R. Evans wrote, for example, "should be fashioned after an ancient temple—partly Jewish, partly Egyptian, for Solomon's Temple partook of both features . . . I rejoice in the building of the Consistory at Meridian, Mississippi . . . It is an Egyptian Temple, so modernized as to admit light into its rooms without destroying that weird effect peculiar to this style of architecture" [36] (FIG. 21). Harry Percy Knowles, New York State's most famous Masonic architect of the period, disagreed; he referred to Masonic temples built in the Egyptian style as "aberrations" and claimed that such buildings "look more like morgues or jails than the homes of an organization whose object is the uplift and betterment of its members." [37]

In 1910 George Fleming Moore, an editor of the *New Age* who later became Sovereign Grand Commander of the Southern Jurisdiction, declared Gothic architecture the most appropriate style and buttressed his argument by quoting Albert Mackey, a leading Masonic scholar of the nineteenth century. "Of all the styles of architecture," Moore claimed, "the Gothic is that which is most intimately connected with the history of Freemasonry, having been the system peculiarly practiced by the Freemasons of the Middle Ages." [38] Evans also noted that a Gothic motif was suitable since it was "in keeping with the meeting place of Knights Templars—those who went to protect pilgrims to the Holy Sepulchre and came back from the Orient embued with the esoteric philosophy of the East." [39] This common perception resulted in scores of Gothic Scottish Rite cathedrals across the country, including George F. Schreiber's spectacular design erected in Indianapolis between 1927 and 1929 (FIG. 4). [40]

The renowned New York architect Harvey Wiley Corbett, a member of Sagamore Lodge No. 371, believed that the Greco-Roman style most adequately met the needs of the fraternity.

47

FIG · 22
Scottish Rite cathedral, San Antonio, Texas, the
Herbert M. Greene Co., architects, 1922–25.
Courtesy of the Livingston Masonic Library,
New York, NY

He claimed that Greek architecture was a refinement of Egyptian forms. The Romans, in turn, added their own "culture and ingenuity," creating "a distinctive style of great beauty and dignity." Supporting the use of classical architecture, he argued, "is a tradition of evolution taking it back to the earliest springs of the Christian religion, so that it represents a style perfectly appropriate to the idea to be expressed."[41] To illustrate Corbett's argument, and to represent the style most commonly employed for Scottish Rite buildings, the *New York Masonic Outlook* published an image of the San Antonio Scottish Rite cathedral, designed by the Herbert M. Greene Company of Dallas, Texas (FIG. 22).[42]

In each of these instances, whether Egyptian, Gothic, or classical, the architectural style associated the Scottish Rite membership with earlier carriers of a mystical, esoteric tradition. This identification explains why the descriptive term *cathedral* often is applied to Scottish Rite meeting spaces, be they separate buildings or simply rooms within larger Masonic temples. As historian Anthony D. Fels has noted, the Scottish Rite was reputed to be the intellectual and mystical branch of the fraternity.[43]

### Archetypes

By participating in the Scottish Rite and allowing himself to be schooled in the esoteric traditions, a member assumed the archetypical role of holy man or priest; he transformed himself into a wise man initiated into the sacred knowledge of the ages. This role functioned complementarily with the paradigmatic identifications of the other three branches of Freemasonry. Within the Blue Lodge's room, a man became a builder or workman. As a Masonic Knight Templar, meeting in a drill hall or so-called asylum, he occupied the role of holy warrior. In the Ancient Arabic Order of Nobles of the Mystic Shrine, with its overlay of jokes and buffoonery, the membership experimented with the role of jester or fool.

By holding overlapping memberships in all these bodies, imbibing their tenets and teachings, and inhabiting their distinct ceremonial spaces, a Mason was presented with a repertoire of

48

103494

complementary identities. No one of these fraternal archetypes provided a complete, well-rounded persona, but the American male could assimilate attitudes and patterns of behavior from each of them. Functioning like anthropologist Levi-Strauss's classic *bricoleur*, he could thus construct a whole man.[44] In 1921 the editor of the *Crescent*, a magazine by and for Shriners, described how the different Masonic groups supplemented each other. "Shrinedom is . . . a place for York Rite and Scottish Rite Masons to relax after receiving the solemn and very sacred assignment to world duty imposed . . . by those bodies," he wrote. "After a man comes through either of those rites he is apt to step around the world for a few months making as much noise as a cat on a Brussels carpet. He is attending a funeral within his brain and soul . . . The Shrine is there to help him back to normalcy."[45]

Within the largest Masonic temples, like George Mason's enormous building in Detroit, each of these four organizations maintained its own quarters. In other cities, such as Peoria, Illinois, the different Masonic bodies constructed separate structures. By inhabiting the lodge room, the drill hall, the cathedral, and the mosque, American men provided themselves with forums where they could express different facets of their personalities. On separate nights within these spaces, they assumed distinct but complementary identities. Back in the workaday world, the priest, soldier, jester, and craftsman were integrated within each individual to form a comprehensive conception of American masculinity.

49

## ⍄ ⊙ T E S

[1] William D. Moore, "American Shriners' Mosques, 1904–1930: Theaters for the Enactment of the Fraternal Other," paper presented at the 48th annual meeting of the Society of Architectural Historians, Seattle, WA, April 7, 1995.

[2] S. Brent Morris shows that Scottish Rite membership went from 39,928 in 1900 to 500,000 in the 1920s in "From Boom to Bust," in *A Radical in the East* (Ames, IA: Iowa Research Lodge No. 2, 1993), 9–34.

[3] For a discussion of the dialectical relationship between humans and objects, see Peter L. Berger, *The Sacred Canopy: Elements of a Sociological Theory of Religion* (Garden City, NY: Doubleday, 1967), 6–10.

[4] The following discussion of the Masonic lodge room of the first three degrees is an abbreviated version of the argument developed in William D. Moore, "The Masonic Lodge Room, 1870–1930: A Sacred Space of Masculine Spiritual Hierarchy," in *Gender, Class, and Shelter: Perspectives in Vernacular Architecture*, V, Elizabeth Collins Cromley and Carter L. Hudgins, eds. (Knoxville: University of Tennessee Press, 1995), 26–39.

[5] Malcolm C. Duncan, *Duncan's Masonic Ritual and Monitor* (New York: Dick & Fitzgerald, 1866).

[6] In 1874 Christopher G. Fox, Grand Master of Masons in New York State, wrote, "I do not like that idea of holding Lodge meetings in the second story of a building, except under circumstances which will warrant its use with absolute security from outside observation either of voice or vision. Unless the building...can be ventilated in such a way as to keep the windows and other openings on the second story closed, especially in the summer season, I am inclined to think that it will not do for a Lodge Room." Letter from Fox to J. R. Mills, January 29, 1874. Photocopy in the file of Fellowship Lodge No. 749, Livingston Masonic Library, New York, NY.

[7] For a discussion of Masonic furniture, see William D. Moore, "Selling the Sacred: Masonic Lodge Rooms, Their Furnishings and Business, 1870–1930," in *Emerging Scholars in American Art: Proceedings from the First Annual Symposium*, Edward S. Cooke, Jr., ed. (Boston: Department of American Decorative Arts and Sculpture, Museum of Fine Arts, 1994), 137–79.

[8] For example, the lodge room in the Masonic temple built in Duluth, Minnesota, in 1890 included a balcony, as did the cathedral room of the Masonic temple built in Spokane, Washington, in 1903. See Duane E. Anderson, *Early Historical Highlights of the Scottish Rite Bodies in the Valley of Duluth*, Orient of Minnesota (Duluth: no pub., no date), 8–9; Frederick E. Michaels, "The Masonic Temple, Spokane, Washington," *The New Age* 9(2) (August 1908), 172–75.

[9] For an explication of contemporaneous Masonic belief, see, for example, H.L. Haywood, *Symbolical Masonry* (Kingsport, TN: Southern Publishers, 1923), 19–25; *Celebration of the Semi-Centennial of Utica Commandery*, N. 3 K. T. (Utica, NY: White & Floyd, 1874), 18–19.

[10] Charles T. McClenachan, *The Book of the Ancient and Accepted Scottish Rite of Freemasonry* (New York: Masonic Publishing and Manufacturing Co., 1867).

[11] *The Secret Directory*.

[12] See Jonathan Blanchard, *Scotch Rite Masonic Illustrated*, 2 vols.(Chicago: Ezra Cook, 1892).

[13] McClenachan, 99, 152, 186, 197, 326, 334, 419.

[14] See, for example, Arthur Andersen and Leon O. Whitsell, *California's First Century of Scottish Rite Masonry* (Oakland: n.p., 1962), 32, 107; "Masonry in Southern California," *The Los Angeles Freemason and Western Mason* 13 (3) (Dec. 1908), 91.

[15] T. W. Hugo, "Daniel Greysolon du Lhut: Duluth and Its Scottish Rite Masonry," *The New Age* 9(4) (Oct. 1908), 378.

[16] James David Carter, *The First Century of Scottish Rite Masonry in Texas, 1867–1967* (Waco: The Texas Scottish Rite Bodies, 1967), 159.

[17] See, for example, the Lilley Co.'s *Ancient and Accepted Scottish Rite of Freemasonry, Northern Jurisdiction, Catalog No. 270* (Columbus, OH: M.C. Lilley & Co., n.d.). For a history of one of the leading regalia firms, see William D. Moore, "M.C. Lilley & Company: Manufacturers of Masonic Furniture," *The Scottish Rite Journal* 100 (9) (Sept. 1992), 59–64.

[18] For a retelling and analysis of the ritual of the first three degrees, see Anthony D. Fels, "The Square and Compass: San Francisco's Freemasons and American Religion, 1870–1900," Ph.D. diss. (Palo Alto, CA: Stanford University, 1987), 143–93.

[19] *Masonic Temple Hand Book* (Chicago: Masonic Fraternity Temple Assn., n.d.), n.p.

[20] Charles E. Rosenbaum, "Albert Pike Consistory, Little Rock, Arkansas," *The New Age* 1 (5) (Aug.–Sept. 1904), 289.

[21] Robert E. McDowell, "Scottish Rite Masonry in South Dakota and the New Temple at Yankton," *The New Age* 4 (3) (March 1906), 268.

[22] Ibid.

[23] James D. Carter, *History of the Supreme Council: Ancient and Accepted Scottish Rite of Freemasonry, Southern Jurisdiction* (Washington, DC: The Supreme Council), 161.

[24] "The Scottish Rite in St. Louis," *Missouri Freemason* (undated clipping in the files of the Livingston Masonic Library, New York, NY).

[25] For a discussion of fairs held to raise funds for the construction of Masonic temples, see William D. Moore, "Funding the Temples of Masculinity: Women's Roles in Masonic Fairs in New York State, 1870–1930," *Nineteenth Century* 14 (1) (1994), 19–25.

[26] "Freemasons as Builders: Scottish Rite Temple at Ft. Wayne, Ind.," *The Builder* 2 (3) (March 1916), 77–79.

[27] Day Allen Willey, "Scottish Rite Temple at Los Angeles," *The New Age* 7(5) (Nov. 1907), 550.

[28] Willey, 551; "The Scottish Rite Cathedral," *The Los Angeles Freemason* 9(11) (Aug. 1905), 330.

[29] "The New Home of the Scottish Rite: Great Cathedral is Artistic Triumph," *Masonic News* 8(7) (July 1927), 15.

[30] "Notes on the Preliminary Studies for the Great Masonic Temple at Detroit," *Architecture* 46(3) (Sept. 1922), 265–72.

[31] James B. Steiner and James W. Skelly, *History of the Scottish Rite Valley of St. Louis Orient of Missouri* (St. Louis, MO: The Valley, 1950), 196.

[32] Codex, "The Stage in Masonry," *The New Age* 4(4) (April 1906), 379.

[33] H.R. Evans, "Lodge Furnishings and Degrees," *The Builder* 2(7) (July 1916), 207.

[34] Francis H. E. O'Donnell, "Philosophy and the Drama in Freemasonry," *The New Age* 4(5) (May 1906), 475–76.

[35] For one of the most fully articulated examples of this line of thinking, see Charles H. Vail, *The Ancient Mysteries and Modern Masonry* (New York: Macoy Publishing and Masonic Supply Co., 1909); see also "Mystery in Masonry," *Southwestern Freemason* 29(5) (May 1925), 1.

[36] Evans, 208.

[37] "Some California Masonic Temples," *The Architect and Engineer of California* 52(2) (Feb. 1918), 56.

[38] George Fleming Moore, "A Great, Gothic Door for a Great Building," *The New Age* (March 1910), 161.

[39] Evans, 208.

[40] Charles E. Crawford, "The Scottish Rite Cathedral at Indianapolis," *Masonic Craftsman* (March 1930), 119–22; *Diamond Jubilee Ancient Accepted Scottish Rite of Freemasonry* (Indianapolis: Scottish Rite Valley of Indianapolis, 1940), 12–14.

[41] Harvey Wiley Corbett, "What Design for the Temple," *New York Masonic Outlook* 4(3) (Nov. 1927), 70. For a discussion of Corbett's Masonic reconstruction of Solomon's temple for the Sesquicentennial Exposition in Philadelphia, see William D. Moore, "Solomon's Temple in America?," *The Northern Light* 24(3) (Aug. 1993), 8–9.

[42] "Two Examples of Rendering by Hugh Ferris," *American Architect* 120(2381)(Nov. 23, 1921), 401; Carter, 305–13.

[43] Fels, 136, 206.

[44] For a discussion of the *bricoleur*, see Claude Levi-Strauss, *The Raw and the Cooked*, translated by John and Doreen Weightmann (New York: Harper & Row, 1962).

[45] *The Crescent* 12(4)(June 1921), 16.

# ⊕ in the scottish rite

## MARY ANN CLAWSON

Spectatorship and masculinity

FIG·1
This postcard depicts a scene of "Christ Before Herod" from an early-twentieth-century unknown play or popular entertainment. The caption on the card reads, "Pilate, in the attempt to evade responsibility, sent Jesus to Herod, who asked for a miracle, and when Jesus refused to work one for his amusement sent him back to Pilate."

**F**RATERNAL ORDERS ARE DISTINGUISHED FROM OTHER SOCIAL ORGANIZATIONS BY THEIR USE OF ELABORATE RITUALS AND DEGREES, OR LEVELS OF MEMBERSHIP, TO INCULCATE MORALITY. Through ritual, men were incorporated into a brotherhood dedicated to ethical instruction. Moreover, the members' ascension through a hierarchy of degrees suggests how enlightenment and self-improvement could be achieved by means of sustained effort over time.

Organizations working within a Masonic model derived much of their cultural authority from these moral claims. As a result, recent scholarship on nineteenth-century fraternalism often places it in a religious context. [1] But fraternal ritual should also be seen as a form of participatory theatre and a systematically marketed entertainment genre. Fraternal orders operated in a market situation, competing with one another and with other ways of spending leisure time and disposable income. Somehow organizational leaders had to resolve the tension between the drive for expansion and the vision of the order as a system of spiritual and moral enlightenment. In this contradictory process, the role of the ritual was central.

In one sense, the ritual, a secret performance, was the means by which the order expressed moral authority over its members and asserted their oneness. At the same time, it was a major incentive to membership. Both the multiplication of Masonic degrees in the late eighteenth century and the search for exciting rituals in the late nineteenth suggest that for many men the high point of fraternal participation was the opportunity to play these dramatic roles. In many orders, rituals were written and rewritten with the goal of attracting members and then discarded if they failed to so. Almost every order engaged in revision: the Odd Fellows in 1835, 1845, and 1880 and the Knights of Pythias in 1866, 1882, and 1892. [2]

Competition among fraternal orders increased in the late nineteenth century, when popular amusements became more numerous, professional, and attractive (FIG. 1). Scottish Rite Masons responded by developing the most elaborate of all fraternal rituals. The result was a curious hybrid that used staged performance to build and sustain a social organization rather than to entertain a mass audience.

## Early History of the Scottish Rite

In eighteenth-century France, enthusiasm for Masonic ceremonies led to a proliferation of esoteric degrees. Through what was titled Scotch, or chivalric, Masonry, initiates could claim the guise of Crusader knights seeking to rebuild the Temple in the Holy Land. Templarism thus deemphasized Masonry's craft ancestry in favor of a myth of aristocratic origin.

Established in Charleston, South Carolina, in 1801, the Scottish Rite is a twenty-nine-degree system constituted around a selection of these "higher" degrees. Within the United States, two autonomous, geographically defined bodies governed Scottish Rite Masonry. The Southern Jurisdiction, the original body, was and is composed of the southern states east of the Mississippi River plus all the states to the west; the Northern Jurisdiction, established in 1813, includes the area north of the Mason-Dixon Line and east of the Mississippi.

Consistent with Masonic tradition, Scottish Rite degrees are dramatically rendered lessons in morality and ethics. At the same time, elaborate titles and exotic locales promise an experience of mystery and exaltation. The eighteenth-century French degrees apparently provided such dramatic pleasures to their participants, but the higher degrees in early-nineteenth-century America were attenuated versions of their continental predecessors, skeletal collections of responsive readings that could be read aloud to an initiate in a single evening. [3]

In 1855 Albert Mackey, the noted Masonic publisher and promoter, invited Albert Pike, a newspaper editor, lawyer, amateur poet, and adventurer, to participate in a revision of the Scottish Rite. Pike devoted more than a decade to developing an elaborately scripted two-volume dramatization of the twenty-nine degrees. By 1867 Charles McClenahan had produced a similarly detailed version for use by the Northern Jurisdiction. The two rituals differ in detail but follow the same basic outline of twenty-nine degrees set largely in the Middle East: King Solomon's temple, the palaces of King Cyrus and King Darius, the desert near Sinai, the court of Saladin, the lodge of Crusader knights (FIGS. 2–4). Within each setting, a heroic figure, representing a Masonic presence, reveals a universal moral truth. Masons are thus portrayed as a moral elite arising throughout.

During most of the nineteenth century, the Scottish Rite was a minor segment of the larger Masonic world, small and obscure in comparison with the York, or American, Rite, the other major system of Masonic higher degrees. In the Southern Jurisdiction, for example, the number of thirty-second-degree Scottish Rite Masons in 1890 was 1,505 compared with 28,467 Knights Templar, the highest level of the York Rite. [4] An order of Christian knighthood, the Knights Templar influenced the formation of numerous other fraternal military organizations, such as the Odd Fellows' Patriarchs Militant. Their Triennial Conclaves attracted public attention when parade units and drill teams clad in military garb marched in formation through the streets of that year's host city.

54

FIG·2
The Great Western Stage Equipment Company
of Kansas City, Missouri, created this sketch for use
in the sixth degree. The image of Solomon's
throne room is indicated in two layers, with the
backdrop appearing in color and the cut drop
that frames the baldachino, or canopy, sketched in
pen and ink. Courtesy of the Performing Arts
Archives of the University of Minnesota Libraries

FIG·3
The Volland Scenic Studio of St. Louis produced
this sketch to create the throne room of
King Cyrus of Persia from the fifteenth degree.
Courtesy of C. Michael Volland, Volland Scenic
Studios, St. Louis, MO

FIG·4
The Sosman and Landis Scene Painting Studios of
Chicago created this cathedral scenery in 1908
for the Scottish Rite temple in Duluth, Minnesota.
Courtesy of the Scottish Rite Bodies of
Duluth, MN

FIG · 5
A postcard of "First Prize Won by Drill Corps of Colorado Commandery No. 1, K[nights]. T[emplar]. at the Triennial Conclave at Louisville, Kentucky, August, 1901—Value $4500.00."
Courtesy of the Library of the Museum of Our National Heritage, Lexington, MA

FIG · 6
The St. Paul Commandery No. 40 from North Adams, Massachusetts, participating in the Knights Templar Triennial Conclave in Boston, 1895. From *Photo Souvenir: 26th Triennial Conclave, Boston 1895.* Courtesy of the Library of the House of the Temple, Washington D.C.

By the early 1900s, however, the Scottish Rite was growing dramatically, increasing from 40,000 members north and south in 1900 to 590,000 by 1927, a point when growth of the York Rite had begun to stall. [5] Masonic historian S. Brent Morris has suggested that the Scottish Rite's more flexible methods of degree conferral, coupled with its concentration in urban areas, in contrast to the more dispersed bodies of the York Rite, explain this shift of influence. But it should also be noted that the order's period of explosive growth coincides precisely with the emergence of the staged ritual as the Scottish Rite's most distinctive feature.

### Transformation: From Lodge Room to Stage

The best way to understand the changes instituted by the Scottish Rite is to examine the degree initiations of Blue Lodge Masonry, which formed the model for almost all other lodge rituals. Initiation took place at the center of the large, rectangular lodge room, as officers and brothers looked on. As William D. Moore points out in his essay, rectangular seating meant that brothers faced each other, their eyes constantly resting on the assemblage of known individuals who constituted the lodge. [6]

A single Scottish Rite degree could have up to four scenes, each calling for a specific decor and props. To avoid the cumbersome process of setting up and dismantling each scene during the ceremony, the lodge room was divided into discrete areas called apartments. The fifteenth degree, for example, the Knight of the East, called for three settings: the Grand Lodge of Perfection at Jerusalem, the interior of the palace of King Cyrus of Persia, and a bridge (FIGS. 3, 8). The king's

56

palace was to be "decorated according to the usual custom of the Orientals," "brilliantly lighted" with
an elevated throne and a transparency or other visual representation of Cyrus's dream. The enactors
would be elaborately costumed to match the splendor of the setting. The Grand High Priest, for example, was to wear "a figured tunic of white linen," a purple robe "upon the border of which are suspended seventy-two small bells, and as many pomegranates, alternating," a breastplate containing
twelve precious stones, and "a purple or blue linen tiara" adorned with a gold plate[7] (FIGS. 9, 10).

     In the fifteenth degree, the initiate, playing Zerubbabel, seeks admission to the Grand
Lodge of Perfection. "A Prince of the house of Judah," he wishes to be created a Knight of the East;
this will enable him to claim from Cyrus, king of Persia, his promise to set free the children of Israel
and allow them to return to Jerusalem to rebuild the temple. In the second scene, Zerubbabel, having

57

**FIG · 9**

This costume for the High Priest was used in the ritual of the Independent Order of Odd Fellows. From the I.O.O.F. catalog #5, 1910s. Courtesy of the Library of the Museum of Our National Heritage, Lexington, MA

**FIG · 10**

High Priest William Fowler from Ancient Chapter No. 1, or York Rite, dated 1875. Courtesy of the Livingston Masonic Library, New York, NY

returned to Persia, is taken prisoner and bound in chains. Presented to the king, played by the lodge's Sovereign Master, he refuses to communicate the secrets of the Jewish masons: "If liberty is to be obtained at such a price, I would prefer an honorable exile or a glorious death."[8] Inspired by his bravery, Cyrus frees both Zerubbabel and the children of Israel. But on the way back, guards accost Zerubbabel and try to rob him of the sword, apron, and sash that Cyrus had bestowed upon him. Besting them in battle, he crosses the bridge and arrives, symbolically, in the holy city.

This summary account suggests both the dramatic possibilities and limitations of degree ritual. A classic initiation drama, it subjects the candidate to tests of bravery and honor through which he earns admission to a higher state of being. The requirements of secrecy prevented the candidate from learning his lines in advance; in some instances, he was given lines to read during the ritual, while in others, the master of ceremonies would act as a stand-in, speaking for the candidate, who stood mute at his side. Although the initiate was, therefore, a somewhat passive figure in this drama, he was positioned at its center. Fully costumed, he was bound in chains, fought a battle, and was invested with the signs, handshakes, and jewels of the degree. He moved through space, from one apartment to the other, and had physical contact with the officers of the lodge as they guided him through the ritual.

Scottish Rite initiation was intended to be a dazzling experience for the initiate, yet few if any local organizations had the resources to administer more than a few fully acted-out degrees. Instead, most degrees were "communicated"—that is, simply read—to the initiate. "Conferral" was the more ambitious and costly dramatized version, calling for the use of props, special effects, and costumes, all of which were available from fraternal-regalia companies as early as the 1870s.

Despite the expedient of communicating most degrees, problems remained; indeed, the rapid communication of numerous degrees often lead to dissatisfaction with the quality of ritual experience. By the mid-1890s, Scottish Rite Masons in many western and southwestern Valleys began to present their rituals as staged dramatic events. And by 1910, many, if not all, Scottish Rite temples and cathedrals had adopted the following changes.

*1.* Candidates were initiated in groups, usually twice a year, at events called reunions. Lasting from three to four days, reunions alternated the conferral of degrees during morning, afternoon, and evening sessions with the provision of meals and socializing in temples or cathedrals owned or controlled by the Scottish Rite.

*2.* Initiations were no longer carried out in traditional rectangular lodge rooms. Instead, the most active Scottish Rite organizations had constructed auditoriums with fully equipped proscenium stages for the presentation of a performed ritual. The initiates now sat as an audience and viewed the initiation rites from a distance.

F I G · 1 1

This "playbill" lists performers for the nineteenth and twentieth degrees from the *Twentieth Century Jubilee Program of the Ancient and Accepted Scottish Rite*, Valley of Wichita, Kansas, April 15–18, 1901. Courtesy of the Scottish Rite Bodies of Wichita, KS

To be Good men and true, and faithfully to keep our secrets, is the first lesson we are taught in our mysteries; that only through fidelity to our obligations and perseverance amid difficulties and reverses, can we build our lives and be worthy of honor and trust.

15TH DEGREE • KNIGHT OF THE EAST

**3.** An improved standard of performance accompanied this reorganization. Participants now memorized rather than read their lines, and temples prided themselves on the magnificence of their costumes, sets, and special effects.

The shift from the traditional lodge room to the auditorium boldly declared to members that the ritual was, among other things, a work of theatre. The earlier lodge-room initiation was also a dramatic event, but it was a performance that emphasized direct participation of candidates. The new separation of performers and onlookers, the recognition of initiates as an audience, and the use of elaborate effects to create a theatre of illusion transformed Scottish Rite enactments into something like a popular entertainment.

Indeed, Scottish Rite participants quickly defined their activities as theatrical in nature. Even in the 1890s, when the earliest stagings occurred in Arkansas and Kansas, reunion programs resembling theatre playbills listed the names of exemplars under the heading "dramatis personae" (FIG. 11). References to directors and to "Masonic actors" appeared by the early 1900s. [9] And commercial theatre operated as an explicit frame of reference and standard of comparison: "Not a theatre in the City [of San Francisco] has so complete and thorough an electrical equipment"; "the massive auditorium [of Wichita, Kansas] is considered as fine, according to its size, as any modern metropolitan theatre in the country." [10] Scottish Rite ritualists almost certainly based their innovations in staging on a prior familiarity with professional-theatre productions.

The turn of the century was a pivotal time in the history of American entertainment. "By the early decades of the twentieth century, the dominant categories for the organization of many of the leading performing arts and entertainments and the terms in which audiences approached them had all been firmly established." [11] The Scottish Rite evolved within this context, and its rituals assumed a hybrid quality, as the fraternity assimilated many of the new trends while defining itself in opposition to others.

### Theatrical Context of Scottish Rite Drama

The American theatrical experience changed significantly during the nineteenth century. The increasing professionalism of performance, the "disciplining" of audiences, and the growing importance of women as a major target for commercial entertainment are all components of what is often referred to as the move from the social audience to the audience of spectatorship. [12] In the Jacksonian era, the theatre had been as much a site for socializing as for involvement with narrative drama. Predominantly male audiences, composed of both middle- and working-class men, used the theatre for talking, drinking, gambling, and assignations with prostitutes, who were often the only women present. Theatregoers weren't expected to come on time or pay strict attention to the perfor-

60

detail from playbill list

**19° Pontiff**

(DRAMATIS PERSONAE)

Grand Pontiff . . . . . . . . . . . . . . .Isaac Goldsmith, 32°
Senior Prelate . . . . . . . . . . . . . . . . . E. L. Martling, 32°
Junior Prelate . . . . . . . . . . . . . . . . Geo. T. Walker, 32°
Orator . . . . . . . . . . . . . . . . . . . . . . . Paul Brown, 32°
Senior Deacon . . . . . . . . . . . . . . . J. H. Reynolds, 32°
Junior Deacon . . . . . . . . . . . . . . . . . . . F. R. Dyer, 32°
Philetus . . . . . . . . . . . . . . . . . . . . Bruce M. Priddy, 32°
Hermes . . . . . . . . . . . . . . . . . . . . . . . . . . I. W. Gill, 32°
Manu . . . . . . . . . . . . . . . . . . . . . . . . . W. R. Tucker, 32°
Philo . . . . . . . . . . . . . . . . . . . . . . . J. A. Rummell, 32°
John . . . . . . . . . . . . . . . . . . . . . . . W. H. Harrison, 32°
Spirit of Darkness . . . . . . . . . . . . . . . J. E. Luling, 32°
Spirit of Masonry . . . . . . . . . Henry Wallenstein, 33°

mance. But when they did attend to the play, boisterous audience members expressed their views vociferously, applauding, booing, and pelting the stage with everything from garbage to furniture. In this age of "audience sovereignty," theatre patrons sometimes stopped the performance altogether or forced the actors to repeat especially popular scenes or passages.

More than an aggregation of anonymous individuals, the early-nineteenth-century audience was a highly interactive social body. By mid-century, however, the conventions and experience of theatregoing had been decisively transformed. The staged Scottish Rite ritual emerged in the wake of two major, interrelated changes in the post–Civil War theatre: the imposition of decorum and the feminization of theatre audiences.

Etiquette books advocated new standards of propriety for theatregoers: "Perfect quiet," one advised, "should be maintained during the performance, and the attention should be fixed on the stage. To whisper or do anything during the performance to disturb . . . others is rude in the extreme."[13] Accordingly, theatre managers attempted to control audience behavior by prohibiting drinking and gaming, by using ushers to enforce promptness and silence, and by reconfiguring the seating so that the pit, with its traditions of working-class rowdyism, became the orchestra section, where genteel patrons occupied fixed, padded seats.

Most importantly, plays were now presented in a darkened theatre, with lighting fixed on the stage. This focused attention on the performance and made it harder for audience members to see and speak to each other. Theatre thus became less a social and more a spectatorial event. "The practice of darkening the theater and the imposition of rules of silence in the decades after the Civil War left audiences with little else to do but consume the entertainment."[14] Simultaneously, the entertainment itself was frequently more compelling, thanks to a higher standard of performance, an emphasis on spectacular stage effects, and the emergence of "stars" to engage the audience's imagination.

The shift toward gentility and decorum was also an attack on the theatre as a men's club. Entrepreneurs who initially realized that the presence of women guaranteed the respectability of their theatres now recognized them as a lucrative new market. By 1900 they constituted a major audience presence at vaudeville shows, now promoted as family entertainment, and at legitimate-theatre performances, increasingly defined as the special province of women audiences. "Our matinee audiences," wrote drama critic Clayton Hamilton in 1911, "are composed almost entirely of women, and our evening audiences are composed of women also, and the men that they brought with them."[15] As narrative drama became identified with largely female audiences, men increasingly sought alternative entertainments such as variety theatre, burlesque, and sporting events.

These changes—the professionalization of theatrical presentation and the disciplining and reconfiguration of the audience—had contradictory consequences. On the one hand, they raised

61

FIG · 12
Beards and wigs available to complete the
costume and character, from catalog #122, *Ancient
and Accepted Scottish Rite Supplies: Southern
Jurisdiction,* C. E. Ward, New London, OH, no date.

FIG · 13

These costumes were available in 1896 from the Henderson-Ames Company for use in the Scottish Rite degrees. An inscription on the introduction page of the catalog reads:

*Red Cross Costumes Award. Our Exhibit at the World's Fair [Columbian Exposition, Chicago: 1893] was awarded the Medal and Diploma for super-excellence of quality and design. To the Jury of Awards our goods recommended themselves as they have to thousands of purchasers, heretofore, as unequaled by any American manufacturer. In every article we manufacture is exemplified the taste of an artist, combined with the skill of expert workmanship, and, as a result, we are leaders in designs, and pride ourselves on the many competitions we have won.*

standards of artistic excellence and facilitated "a more intense collaboration" between performers and audiences, "perhaps even a moment of spiritual communion in which both were enlarged." On the other, they may have resulted in a "loss of a communal and amateur spirit of participation, with a greater engagement with the dramatic text purchased at the price of a more privatized, passive, and isolating experience typical of the emerging culture of consumption." "Audiences," John Kasson writes, "increasingly viewed performers as across a gulf, and one another as strangers." [16]

In many ways, the evolving Scottish Rite rituals reflected these changes. Improved performance standards and the cultivation of spectacle generated enormous growth. But they also raised questions about the implications of the staged ritual for the Scottish Rite as a Masonic institution, questions centering on three concerns: spectatorship versus social cohesion, pleasure and consumption versus Masonic moralism, and the issue of masculinized drama and feminized men.

### *Spectatorship versus Cohesion*

Two aspects of the staged ritual helped create a more spectatorial experience. First, Scottish Rite lodges "embraced the decorative and highly romantic scenery and improved lighting of the late nineteenth century," presenting "a complete visual experience to rival what was available on the best of American stages." [17] This use of elaborate, professionally designed sets and lighting produced an extraordinary visual spectacle that transported the audience from its everyday world.

Second, the relocation of degree enactors from the lodge room to the stage defined them as actors. Their incorporation into a strikingly lit and lavishly staged world of illusion placed them at a physical and symbolic remove from the degree recipients and implicitly raised expectations for their performance (FIG. 12). This may have been particularly important in the Scottish Rite, as a discussion in the Southern Jurisdiction's magazine, *The New Age*, suggests.

In 1907 Epes W. Sargent, a drama critic and thirty-second-degree Mason, argued that the moral and spiritual possibilities of the ritual were not being as fully realized as they might with an improved standard of performance. His observations, based on those Valleys (probably concentrated in the Northern Jurisdiction) where degree rituals were still conducted in lodge rooms, reveal much about the limitations of these enactments. Sargent called for greater attention to historical accuracy, chiding exemplars for their "unwillingness or inability to look after detail," which can only "rob these splendid dramas of half of their effect. . . . Is it natural to suppose that the followers of the Persian court of Darius, the council of King Solomon, the Hebrews in the wilderness, and the court of Frederick the Great were all given to parting their hair in the middle, cutting it short in the back, and wearing high collars and patent leather shoes?" (FIG. 13). Urging the actors to improve their performance, he emphasized their duty to "yield unquestioning obedience to the director and strive with all

63

FIG · 14

earnestness to supplement his work by realizing to the fullest the meaning of the part entrusted to their care." [18]

But even the most committed Masonic actors faced special difficulties, Sargent argued, because they, unlike professionals, "are acting before their friends." While the stage actor can easily disregard an audience of virtual strangers, "the exemplar has no footlight screen to shut him from his audience. If he is at all sensitive to ridicule he is keenly conscious of his fancied ridiculous appearance in costume, and the knowledge that the men who form a part of his daily life are so regarding him does not conduce to ease of manner." [19]

According to this view, the proximity and familiarity of lodge-room exemplification undermined the authority of the ritual. Its movement to a stage seems a clear response to this problem, because theatrical lighting, elaborate sets, and sensational effects distanced the exemplars from the familiar social atmosphere of the lodge-room floor. The increasing size of the twice-yearly reunion classes must also have heightened the division between the audience of initiates and the exemplars on stage, a division Sargent presumably would have applauded.

The logic dictating these changes was that the candidate's loss of a participant's role in the ritual, the creation of barriers between exemplars and recipients, and a more gripping presentation of the ritual would result in a greater focus on the drama, coupled with a more passive, individualized relationship to it. In other words, the spectatorial ideal would triumph over the active sociability of the traditional initiation process. But the Scottish Rite experience was more complex.

The purpose of a commercial play or movie was simply to attract an audience, a collection of anonymous individuals united only by their common willingness to pay the price of admission. [20] In contrast to a theatre audience, with its continual turnover and lack of internal structure, the Scottish Rite was a formal, structured, highly organized group. The purpose of the staged drama was to create a lasting group identification, as well as to encourage the initial affiliation. In these significant ways, the Scottish Rite drama retained the ideal of social audience.

The ritual was presented within the framework of the reunion, a three-to-four-day event in which the conferral of degrees alternated with luncheons, dinners, and late-evening refreshments in the banquet rooms that were as much a part of Scottish Rite temples as were the stages. Reunion programs reveal the importance attached to these meals: "Candidates, attending committees and all officers engaged in the work of conferring the respective Degrees, will be expected to lunch and dine there." Even members not directly involved in the reunion were "earnestly solicited to dine there each evening, and spend a social hour with their Brethren." [21] Thus, the theatrical rituals were repeatedly interrupted by another kind of rite, one of fellowship and conviviality designed to integrate degree recipients into the larger social

16TH DEGREE · PRINCE OF JERUSALEM

64

A photo of the "Alpha One Thousand Class,"
May 1924. Courtesy of the Scottish Rite Bodies of
St. Louis, MO

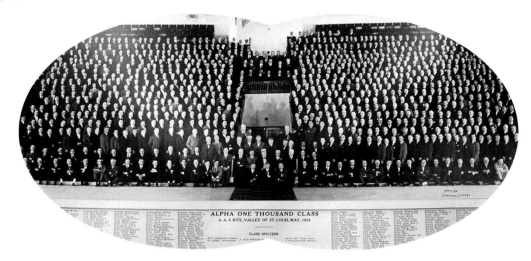

body. In the interludes between performances, they found themselves in a luxurious building resembling a men's club, with a dining hall, smoking rooms and lounges, a library, billiard and card rooms, and a ladies' parlor—features that, as Day Allen Willey wrote of the Los Angeles temple, "make it a favorite gathering place for members of the Scottish Rite who would know each other socially."[22]

The reunion was a sequence of alternating events that continuously pulled the degree recipients back and forth between spectatorship and sociability (FIG. 14). It represented a compromise, combining the camaraderie and collective identity of the traditional fraternal order with the excitement and professionalism of the rapidly expanding world of commercial entertainment. This compromise accorded the Scottish Rite a distinctive character that enhanced its status within the larger fraternal world.

For most within the organization, explosive growth was a powerful argument to implement further ritualistic innovation (FIGS. 15, 16). At the same time, however, some members—possibly those of an older generation who resented their loss of influence—expressed objections. Considered within the context of a more general cultural criticism, their quarrel focused on the emerging consumer society and the new conceptions of masculinity that accompanied it. These naysayers analyzed the dichotomies of duty and pleasure, intellect and sensation, in gender-coded language that both empowered their critique of consumer society and expressed their concern over the "feminization" of the Scottish Rite.

### *Duty versus Pleasure*

In the early 1900s, three Scottish Rite commentators—Francis H. E. O'Donnell, William Knox, and a correspondent who identified himself as Codex—wrote in the *New Age* to decry the abuses of Scottish Rite drama. All three feared that the visual spectacle of the staged ritual was compromising the philosophical integrity of Masonry. "What," asked Codex, "are the rituals for? Why, to teach the aspirant certain lessons in morals and philosophy; to lead him by gradual steps up the great ladder of the Rite, as one leads a scholar in arithmetic to the higher flights of mathematics." Francis O'Donnell similarly argued that Freemasonry was a philosophical system that could only be understood through sustained and disciplined effort. With such goals in mind, the extravagant spectacle of the staged ritual was indeed cause for concern. "Fine acting is a high art productive of pleasing but evanescent results," whereas the proper aim of Masonry is "to give knowledge rather than to please."[23]

William Knox was more scathing, charging that "glorious, spectacular, ornate ritualism" coupled with the prestige of membership were the only factors motivating many to join the Scottish Rite. The "intellectual feasts spread before the brethren by those learned in the doctrine, his-

65

"To him that overcometh will I give to eat of the hidden manna."

The lesson, Repent, keep my commandments, be zealous and faithful, for only the pure in heart shall see God.

tory, and teaching of Masonry" had been replaced, Knox concluded, by "lucid scenic display and strut-tings and mouthings of indifferent amateur actors," with questionable consequences for candidates and for "the institution itself"[24] (FIG. 17).

To these detractors, the ritual had become merely a dramatic spectacle observed by the passive initiates. "The tendency of the time," Codex continued, "is to relegate the onlookers (the Brethren) to mere spectators of a theatrical performance. They are perched in a gallery and have no more to do with the ceremonies of the evening than a man who buys a seat in the dress circle of a the-atre at a grand spectacular show" (FIG. 18). Knox argued that the Scottish Rite was now engaged in the marketing of sensation by means of "moving wires . . . stalking ghosts, diaphanous forms, unearth-ly yells, groans, shrieks, flashing lights, storms, earthquakes." As a result, "selling degrees [was] one of the greatest money-making businesses of the day."[25]

Such commercialization, indicative of the "spirit of the age," was obscuring, if not total-ly corrupting, the "sublime degrees." O'Donnell was more circumspect, but he too warned that drama-tization must always be subordinated to the philosophical content: "An exclusive surrender of Masonic instruction to a dramatic presentation of the rites and ceremonies would be an absolutely certain omen of the decadence of the Order."[26]

### Masculinized Drama or Feminized Men?

For O'Donnell and Codex, the opposition between Masonry as a philosophic system and Masonry as a purveyor of visual pleasure was gender-based, with the elaborately staged ritual rep-resenting the feminization of a masculine system of order and rationality. Initially, this seems a puz-zling interpretation, since the Scottish Rite was unequivocally a males-only organization that con-veyed, through its ritual, a distinctive vision of manly honor. Furthermore—and most strikingly—the written text of the Scottish Rite depicted a world in which women did not exist, physically or themat-ically. This exclusion of women meant that many of the era's most sacred themes (and dependable dra-matic vehicles), such as womanly virtue, a mother's love, and the defense of home and family, were eliminated from the discursive universe of the Rite.

The Scottish Rite depicts men only as *public* figures, as rulers, religious leaders, sol-diers, and so on. Not only are there no women, but there also is no *private* sphere. It is striking, for example, that the only stock scenery found in opera houses but omitted from Masonic outfittings were the kitchens, gardens, and conservatories associated with Victorian depictions of romance and domes-ticity. In this sense, the ritual's content echoed the themes of an earlier era, when playbills were selec-ted to appeal to male audiences, and "manly" virtues were preferred over romance, robust heroes and villains over matinee idols.[27]

FIG · 17

Frederick H. Stuckey, thirty-third degree,
as King Solomon, from the *Twentieth Century Jubilee
Program of the Ancient and Accepted Scottish
Rite*, Valley of Wichita, Kansas, April 15–18, 1901.
Courtesy of the Scottish Rite Bodies of
Wichita, KS

FIG · 18

Photograph from a reunion program of the new
scenery installed by Volland Scenic Studios
of the crucifixion scene from the eighteenth degree
for the Scottish Rite temple in St. Louis, Missouri.
Courtesy of the Library of the House of the
Temple, Washington, D.C.

Spectatorship and Masculinity in the Scottish Rite

By addressing only men and recognizing men alone as moral actors, the Scottish Rite ritual defined masculine identity through a discourse that effaced women and home, two of the era's most potent symbols, and rendered them irrelevant to life's highest truths and noblest contests. The Scottish Rite dramatization can, therefore, be seen as a masculine response to what Richard Butsch has called the "re-gendering" of legitimate theatre, a vehicle by which men attempted to reclaim narrative drama as a masculine activity. At the same time, however, the very process of staging introduced new ambiguities and poses this question: In producing and viewing the staged ritual, were Scottish Rite men reclaiming theatre as a masculine sphere, or were they engaging in an activity that was feminine and feminizing?

The visual exoticism of the staged ritual alarmed the critics. At a time when upstanding men dressed in somber black suits, a love of adornment and a fascination with bedecking oneself or watching others so bedecked were considered effeminate. A mid-nineteenth-century etiquette book advised: "'Don't wear anything that is pretty . . . What have men to do with pretty things?'"[28] But in Scottish Rite drama, men arrayed in dazzling colors and luxuriant robes had everything to do with prettiness. To the extent that the spectacle appealed to men's delight in visual sensation generally and to beauty in particular, it imparted a "feminine" aura.

Codex addressed this issue quite directly in his complaints about "extravagance" of costume, which he linked to the related dangers of Catholicism and effeminacy. Charging that Scottish Rite costumes were patterned after vestments of "the Romish Church," he complained that "we have the clothing of the Lady of Babylon, if we do not have her dogmas." The personification of the Church of Rome as a lady or, more likely, as a whore was linked to Catholicism's ritual vestments, which seemed, to some, suspiciously feminine and in clear contrast to the sober garb of the Protestant clergy. "Slowly and insidiously this Jesuitism is cropping up again. This time in the shape of *man millinary*"—that is, through the appeal of fancy and thus effeminizing dress.[29]

When Francis O'Donnell wrote that the aim of Masonry was "to give knowledge rather than to please," he was clearly calling the Scottish Rite back to its masculine mission, for "to please" was surely the province of "the gentler sex." For O'Donnell, Masonry was a project of masculine regeneration: "Freemasonry works to create an army of Exemplars not Actors. Soldiers of the Light, who by their everyday bearing in business, society and the family, unostentatiously depict the glory of the Better Life—the Moral Manhood amongst Men."[30]

Obviously, Codex and O'Donnell saw the Scottish Rite as threatened by feminization. Yet the Rite's increased economic and organizational investment in an exclusively male performance genre would seem to argue quite the opposite—that the organization stood in opposition to the powerful social trends that cultivated and included women audiences. One explanation of these two visions

FIG · 19

A photograph of the scenery installed in 1902 in the Butte, Montana, Scottish Rite temple by the Volland Scenic Studios of St. Louis, Missouri. The scene depicts the cave used in the ninth degree. Courtesy of the House of the Temple, Washington, D.C.

is that they represent two alternative conceptions of masculinity at a time of social transformation. E. Anthony Rotundo characterizes this as the transition from an ideal of "self-made manhood," in which masculinity is defined through self-discipline and economic achievement, to what he terms "passionate manhood," whereby men are able to cultivate their individuality. Play and leisured entertainment—once considered marks of effeminacy—became approved activities for men as the nineteenth century ended, and consumer choice became a form of male self-expression. A man defined his identity not just in the workplace but through modes of enjoyment and self-fulfillment outside of it. [31]

This embrace of pleasure and consumption is visible in all facets of the early-twentieth-century Scottish Rite experience. Published accounts fairly exult in the opulence of the newly constituted temples and cathedrals, which combined, in their members' eyes, all the best features of a fine men's club and a well-equipped metropolitan theatre. Consider, for example, the yearly Maundy Thursday banquets, obligatory for all Knights Rose Croix. In Butte, Montana, in 1902, the banquet included oysters on the half shell, lobster salad, roast spring lamb with mint sauce, and turkey with calf's foot jelly, accompanied by sauterne, St. Julienne, and burgundy wines. While we can only guess at the difficulty and expense involved in transporting oysters and lobster to Butte, not to mention their questionable condition when they arrived, we can be sure that such a menu was intended to display prestige and extol the pleasures of consumption. Elaborate banqueting in a males-only setting was a practice that shaped class and gender into a single honorific identity (FIG. 19).

A similar interest in consumption is revealed in descriptions of temples that emphasize their "superb costuming, elegant paraphernalia and exquisite scenery and stage equipment." A stage setting was "remarkable for the vividness of its representation," "a landscape so realistic that the spectator can readily imagine he hears the noise of the water falling over the cataract." Equally eloquent accounts describe the banquet rooms and lounges, with their "rich mahogany," "weathered oak," and "cozy corners" in the "old Dutch style," not to mention "the largest Axminster Wilton rug ever woven."[32] Again, a delight in costly and tasteful consumption is palpable, coupled with an attention to detail that Codex or O'Donnell might have seen as suspiciously reminiscent of a women's magazine.

18TH DEGREE • KNIGHT ROSE CROIX

69

*Conclusion*

The critiques of Codex, O'Donnell, and Knox illustrated the tensions produced by alternative conceptions of the Masonic experience: a traditional view of ritual as the exemplification of a system of moral instruction versus its emergent status as a leisure activity. The shift from lodge room to auditorium and from initiates-as-participants to initiates-as-spectators, as well as the use of elaborate stage effects to create a theatre of illusion, placed the Scottish Rite squarely within the expanding realm of popular entertainment and gave it a competitive advantage within the populous fraternal world. Furthermore, as a men's organization it offered dramatic spectacle for a males-only audience at a time when mainstream theatre was increasingly considered a feminine pastime.

These changes within the organization fostered debate about perceptions of manhood. Critics of the dramatized ritual spoke nostalgically for an earlier vision, which emphasized the redeeming qualities of hard work and self-discipline, whether in pursuit of economic gain or Masonic enlightenment. A new view, in which "certain uses of leisure time and certain consumer tastes became markers of manliness," challenged this convention.[55] Pleasure was now defined as a masculine right and privilege, a source of pride. With its combination of enthralling drama, bourgeois comfort, and masculine fellowship, the transformed Scottish Rite exemplified the attractions of this perspective. By redefining itself in terms of spectatorship and consumption, the Scottish Rite achieved both enormous growth and an enhanced prestige within the Masonic world that drowned out the naysayers. "Lay aside your business for the occasion," proclaimed the Little Rock reunion program of 1898. "Be with us and enjoy the fruits of our labor . . . judge for yourself whether or not you have a right to feel gratified and proud that you are a Scottish Rite Mason."

[1] Lynn Dumenil, *Freemasonry and American Culture, 1880–1959* (Princeton: Princeton University Press, 1984); Mark Carnes, *Secret Ritual and Manhood in Victorian America* (New Haven: Yale University Press, 1989); Tony Fels, "Religious Assimilation in a Fraternal Organization: Jews and Freemasonry in Gilded-Age San Francisco," *American Jewish History* 74 (1985). For a more secular interpretation, see Mary Ann Clawson, *Constructing Brotherhood: Class, Gender, and Fraternalism* (Princeton: Princeton University Press, 1989).

[2] See Carnes, *Secret Ritual*, 98–104, for an account of the Improved Order of Red Men's struggle to develop a successful ritual.

[3] James D. Carter, *History of the Supreme Council, 33°, Ancient and Accepted Scottish Rite of Freemasonry Southern Jurisdiction, U.S.A. 1891–1921* (Washington, D.C.: The Supreme Council, 33°, 1971), 159–60.

[4] Ibid., 373–74.

## Π ☉ T E S

[5] S. Brent Morris, "Boom to Bust in the Twentieth Century: Freemasonry and American Fraternities," the 1988 Anson Jones Lecture, presented to the Texas Lodge of Research, March 19, 1988.

[6] William D. Moore, "The Masonic Lodge Room, 1870–1930: A Sacred Space of Masculine Spiritual Hierarchy," a paper presented at the Scottish Rite Planning Conference, Minneapolis, Sept. 12, 1992.

[7] Charles T. McClenachan, *The Book of the Ancient and Accepted Scottish Rite of Freemasonry* (New York, Author's Edition, 1901: The Masonic Publishing Company, 1867), 199–200.

[8] *The Complete Ritual of the Ancient and Accepted Scottish Rite* (Chicago: Ezra A. Cook, 1944), 398.

[9] For example, "Most Masonic actors are not what their professional brothers call quick studies." Epes W. Sargent, "The Player, the Part and the Precept," *The New Age* VI (May 1907), 357.

[10] "The 'California Bodies' of the Ancient and Accepted Scottish Rite of Freemasonry and Their New Home," *The New Age* III (July 1905), 72; *Reunion Program* (Wichita, KS, 1898).

[11] John Kasson, *Rudeness and Civility: Manners in Nineteenth-Century America* (New York: Hill and Wang, 1990), 256.

[12] These changes are described in Robert C. Allen, *Horrible Prettiness: Burlesque and American Culture* (Chapel Hill: University of North Carolina Press, 1991); Richard Butsch, "Bowery B'hoys and Matinee Ladies: The Re-Gendering of Nineteenth-Century American Theater Audiences," *American Quarterly* 46 (Sept. 1994), 374–405; Kasson, *Rudeness and Civility*; and Bruce A. McConachie, "Pacifying American Theatrical Audiences, 1820–1900," in *For Fun and Profit: The Transformation of Leisure into Consumption* (Philadelphia: Temple University Press, 1990).

[13] Quoted in Kasson, 242.

[14] Butsch, 395.

[15] Quoted in Butsch, 395.

[16] Kasson, 255.

[17] C. Lance Brockman, "The Age of Scenic Art: The Nineteenth Century," in *The Twin City Scenic Collection: Popular Entertainment 1895–1929* (Minneapolis: University of Minnesota Art Museum, 1987), 7.

[18] Epes W. Sargent, "Detail and the Drama of the Degree," *The New Age* VII (April 1907), 175, 177.

[19] Sargent, "Player," 357.

[20] Robert C. Allen and Douglas Gomery, *Film History: Theory and Practice* (New York: Alfred K. Knopf, 1985), 156.

[21] *Reunion Program* (St. Louis, Nov. 11–14, 1902).

[22] Day Allen Willey, "Scottish Rite Temple at Los Angeles," *The New Age* VII (Nov. 1907), 552–53.

[23] Codex, "Innovations in the Ritual," *The New Age* IV (March 1906), 275; Francis E. H. O'Donnell, "Philosophy and the Drama in Freemasonry," *The New Age* IV (May 1906), 477.

[24] William Knox, "What Excuse?," *The New Age* VII (Sept. 1907), 253–54. Knox's reference to "lucid scenic display" may well contain a misprint; "lurid" better accords with the tone and substance of his essay.

[25] Codex, "The Stage in Masonry," *The New Age* IV (April 1906), 379; Knox, "What Excuse?," 252–53.

[26] Knox, 254; O'Donnell, 477.

[27] Butsch, 379–80.

[28] Quoted in Kasson, 118.

[29] Codex, "Stage in Masonry," 379. The term "man-milliner" was made famous by Republican politician Roscoe Conkling's 1877 attack on political reformers. "By using 'man milliner,'" E. Anthony Rotundo notes, "Conkling evoked the idea of a 'man-woman.'" Rotundo, *American Manhood: Transformations in Masculinity from the Revolution to the Modern Era* (New York: Basic Books, 1993), 271.

[30] O'Donnell, 475.

[31] Rotundo, 6.

[32] *Reunion Program* (St. Louis, Nov. 11–14, 1902); Willey, "Los Angeles," 551, 553.

[33] Rotundo, 283.

FIG · 1

This colored sketch, created for the fourth degree, depicts the entrance to "the ineffable degrees" and Solomon's temple, with the symbolic columns of Jachin and Boaz on either side of the **doorway.** Courtesy of C. Michael Volland, Volland Scenic Studios, St. Louis, MO

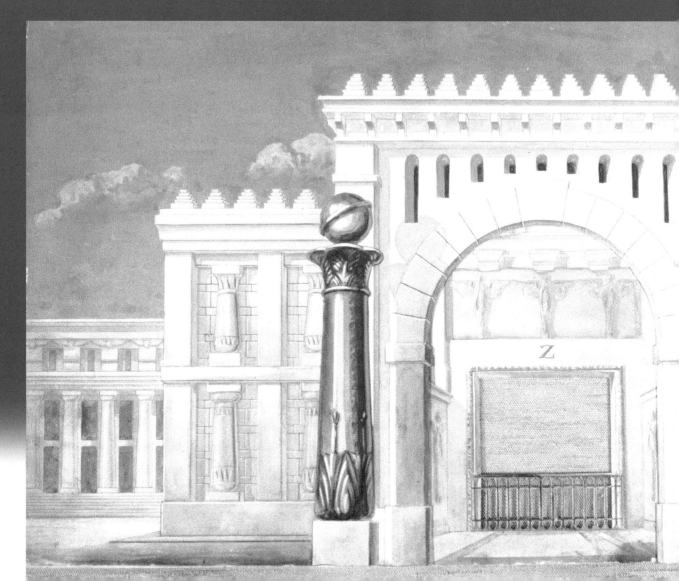

O N WEEKDAY EVENINGS IN LATE-NINETEENTH- AND EARLY-TWENTIETH-CENTURY AMER-
ICA, AFTER THE SUN HAD SET AND WIVES AND CHILDREN HAD REPAIRED TO THEIR
PARLORS, MILLIONS OF MIDDLE-CLASS MEN STREAMED BACK INTO THE BUSINESS DIS-
TRICTS OF THE CITY, BORNE BY HORSE-DRAWN STREETCARS OR COAL-FUELED TRAINS
AWAY FROM THE PREDICTABLE PLEASURES OF DOMESTIC LIFE. If only for a few hours, the men were
escaping into the darkness toward the heart of the city. As they descended from the streetcars and
trains, silhouetted by gaslights or the strange blue hues of the new electric arcs, they called to friends
and associates and gathered in little knots to banter or discuss the affairs of the day: the investigation
of kickbacks in the comptroller's office, the rise in gas-company shares, the scandalous costumes
flaunted at the latest vaudeville show. The jokes were rough and the language unguarded. This was
their world, one they had helped build and whose workings they knew intimately. Within these mighty engines of business, industry, and finance, they were small cogs, to be sure, but cogs with-
out which the engines could not go, or so they believed.

Some of the men, especially those who worked
with tools and machines, veered off toward the Knights of Labor
or the insurance orders, such as the Ancient Order of United
Workmen or the Royal Arcanum. Others—bankers, factory
superintendents, shopkeepers with ambition and drive—proceeded farther into the city, until they were surrounded by soaring
masses of red brick and limestone. Eventually they reached the
two giant columns—Jachin and Boaz—that stood outside the
temple of the Freemasons (FIG.1). And the highest-ranking
Masons, especially those with a facility for memorization, entered
the sacrosanct precincts of the most respected of the orders: the
Ancient and Accepted Scottish Rite of Freemasonry. There they
would participate in an elaborate and astonishingly prolix
sequence of rituals, twenty-nine in all, in which they would be initiated, and initiate others, into the requisite mysteries of becoming thirty-second-degree Masons.

### Reliance on Rituals

What brought these men to the inner sanctum of
Scottish Rite Freemasonry? Perhaps a desire to get away from

home and to cavort with men much like themselves. But they could just have easily, and with considerably more animated pleasure, quaffed a few tankards of beer at the saloon or played billiards or cards at the men's club. Instead, they came to the lodge, where they reenacted stories and legends about ancient gods and goddesses, Old Testament figures, and medieval knights. The central theme of these rituals concerned the assassination of one Hiram Abiff, the master builder of King Solomon's temple and possessor of the pronunciation of the mystical name of God. By participating in these rites, Scottish Rite Freemasons journeyed to distant lands set in the remote past. There, they would restore Hiram to light, avenge his murder, and eventually learn the true mysteries of God.

Their journey began as soon as they entered the anteroom, where they donned the cloaks of shepherds, the extravagant mitres and costumes of Jewish high priests, or the mail and armor of medieval knights (FIG. 2). They arranged the sets and paraphernalia—altars, candles, lighting effects. Then they marched together into the temple itself, an enormous carpeted room with pews along each wall, altars in the center. Mysterious words, warnings, and prayers were uttered, and the lights were extinguished. As if by magic, late-Victorian America gave way to an ancient and exotic realm. A resounding knock on the thick oak door heralded the arrival of an initiate seeking admission to this wondrous world.

Nervous expectation rippled through the temple. The blindfolded initiate (FIG. 3) was gently pulled into the room by a "cable tow" around his neck. Various officers offered prayers and posed cryptic questions and challenges. A lodge officer portraying King Solomon asked whether the candidate should be allowed to "behold the resplendant name of God." Another officer responded that the initiate must first take an oath of secrecy. The initiate recited the oath, and the blindfold was removed. Then a messenger arrived bearing the remains of Hiram Abiff. A group including the initiate marched around the lodge and stopped before an urn containing Hiram's ashes. The candidate, prompted by his conductor, carried the urn to a "sanctuary," while Solomon prayed to the glory of God and the need to obey His will. More instruction on the secret passwords, grips, and signals followed. The initiate set the urn down and listened. Nearly an hour later, the ceremony ended and the lights came on. Another initiate had attained the fourth degree of the Scottish Rite.

This abbreviated rendering of the fourth-degree ritual fails to convey what modern readers might consider its mind-numbing verbosity. The dramatic tension accompanying the arrival of the blindfolded initiate was undercut by the recitation of seemingly endless prayers and dense explications of arcane symbols. What, if anything, it meant to initiates a century ago is hard for us to determine.

In their commentaries on the ritual, Masonic writers warned that most members would indeed be puzzled by the fourth degree. But they agreed on its significance. Albert Pike, the foremost

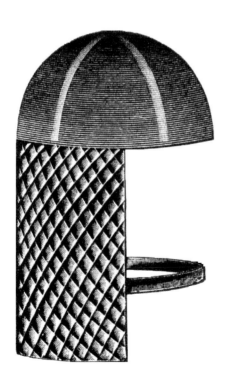

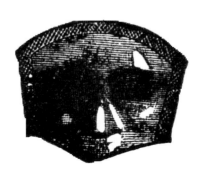

F I G · 4

An interior view of the Sosman and Landis
Scene Painting Studios of Chicago. The backdrops
were painted on frames similar to the one on
the left side of the image. A completed backdrop
was cut off the frame and rolled on hollowed
basswood tubes for shipping by rail to the theatre
or temple. Courtesy of the John R. Rothgeb
Papers, Theatre Arts Collection, Harry Ransom
Humanities Research Center, University of
Texas, Austin


F I G · 5

(opposite below) Sosman and Landis Studios
created this scenery, used in the fourth degree, for
the Scottish Rite temple in Wichita, Kansas,
in 1908. Courtesy of the Scottish Rite Bodies of
Wichita, KS

Masonic ritualist and scholar of the nineteenth century, explained that while the previous three degrees may not have satisfied initiates, greater truths came with the fourth, the "first step toward the inner sanctuary and heart of the temple."[1] And while many of the Scottish Rite rituals were substantially revised and even completely reworked throughout the last half of the nineteenth century, the fourth degree remained virtually unchanged. Since thousands of men spent untold hours memorizing and reenacting it, presumably it meant something to them. Certainly it meant something to others: Hundreds of fraternal orders that proliferated in Victorian America pirated—and then often abbreviated—rituals of the Scottish Rite.

### Visuals Enhance Message

Fraternal rituals generally took place at the center of the lodge room, with the altar serving as focal point. Much of their appeal—and no doubt meaning—was imparted visually. During the late nineteenth century, the Scottish Rite emphasized the visual elements by moving the ceremony from the center of the lodge room to a stage at one end, and initiates merely observed the ritual as others acted it out. This change made it possible to initiate large numbers at one time, but by transforming initiates into spectators, the new procedures threatened to deprive them of the emotional charge of being blindfolded, threatened, and challenged—that is, of experiencing the ritual drama.

The new arrangement required a compelling performance, and Scottish Rite officials relied on increasingly elaborate dramaturgical effects, especially painted backdrops, to intensify the spectators' emotional response (FIG. 4). Companies that had specialized in stage scenery now offered stunning backdrops for all the Scottish Rite rituals, and traveling salesmen marketed these to lodge officials. One such example was the painted backdrop for the fourth degree (FIG. 5), which depicted the interior of King Solomon's temple. The composition of this backdrop, created in 1908 by the Sosman and Landis Scene Painting Studios, was rigidly symmetrical, with massive spare columns holding even more massive lintels that supported an evidently enormous structure. Light pierced two high windows and reflected harshly off smooth stone surfaces or cast menacingly angular, dark shadows. Sharp horizontal and vertical lines intersecting at right angles projected an uncompromising geometrical precision and symmetry. For men who had grown up amid the soft, decorative profusion of Victorian interiors, this representation of Solomon's inner sanctum would have been striking indeed.

A particular designer or painter created the pictured backdrop, but certain significant visual motifs often appeared on other backdrops and in books on the Rite. In addition, the verbal component of the ritual included specific allusions to the visual elements on the backdrop. For example, a square piece of cloth was pinned to the initiate's blindfold. When the initiate was presented to Solomon, the king explained that the "square upon the initiate's forehead" meant that "reason rules his

Peace shall be the universal law for all children of a common father. The True Man and Mason lives and labors for the benefit of those who are to come after him as well as for the advancement of the human race.

Scottish Rite and the Visual Semiotics of Gender

mind." This entitled the initiate to learn how to pronounce the name of God, provided he follow the "straight steps" in the path of the commandments. In Pike's expanded version of the ritual, Solomon explained that the square on the initiate's forehead reminded him to follow the "straight path of virtue" and also to recall that, among ancient philosophers, the square and its "straight lines and angles" denoted the earth, while heavens were signified by means of "great curves and circles."[2]

     The central icons of Freemasonry—the square and the compass—were meant explicitly to teach members the precise regularities of geometry. Accordingly, initiates were ordered during the rituals to place one foot or leg or arm in a perpendicular position, to march in a straight line ("on the level"), and to pivot at sharp right angles. Signals of recognition and distress required strictly vertical, horizontal, or perpendicular hand and finger motions.

     Scottish Rite rituals repeatedly affirmed that the temple of Solomon symbolically represented the "interior and spiritual" life of the initiate, and the visual elements of the degrees seemed to confirm that fraternal members in some way became linked with their visual environment (FIG. 6). The initiate, decorated with a square and invested with the implements of geometry, was to move his body in angular ways, and framed by the linearity of the backdrop, he did so within an environment of extraordinarily jagged lines and angles. To a generation that had learned to think of male and female bodies as possessing antithetical geometrical elements, these dictates seemed quite logical.

     An example is the visual evolution of Jo, the heroine of Louisa May Alcott's *Little Women* (1866). As Jo begins her pilgrimage to adulthood, she is a tomboy, whom Alcott describes as "angular" and hard-edged. But as Jo enters Victorian womanhood, Alcott notes that her character's "angles are much softened," her hair has lengthened into a "thick coil," her eyes have a "soft shine," and her customarily "sharp tongue" has been curbed. Victorian masculinity, on the other hand, was commonly associated with words such as *upright, angular,* and *erect,* and curvilinear body shapes suggested male inadequacy. Theodore Roosevelt, for example, complained in 1897 of effete young men whose shoulders "slope like those of a champagne bottle."[3]

     The association of certain configurations of visual elements—lines, surface textures, mass, and shape—with ideal male and female bodies was reinforced by Victorian fashions. Women's bodies typically were bound in corsets to inscribe curves and then enveloped in layers of soft and intricately decorated materials. Men's clothing, on the other hand, was characterized by well-defined straight lines, sharp angles, plain fabrics, and dark colors.

     Fraternal orders increasingly applied this engendered imagery to ritual spaces within the lodge. And the rituals themselves stated that the temple design symbolized the proper moral and emotional endowments of the initiates. Thus, as initiates marched around the rectangular edges of Solomon's temple, with squares pasted on their foreheads and compass marks on their chests, and as

78

they received instruction in the angular motions and movements associated with the secret recognition signals, they also were receiving subtle lessons in the aesthetics of Victorian masculinity.

### Space Reflects Rituals' Significance

Freemasons assiduously underscored the significance of ritual space within the lodge. Esoteric theories concerning sacred numbers, presumably derived from Jewish mysticism, often governed the design and dimensions of their sacred spaces. The Masonic temple in Peoria, for example, contained rooms that were precisely thirty-three feet in width, height, and length, thirty-three being a number of great esoteric meaning in Freemasonry. Abstract mathematical principles were more obviously incorporated in the movements of actors and members within the temple.

Historian William D. Moore has observed that the ritual activities in nearly all Masonic temples were focused along either of two visual axes. The primary axis ran through the center of the room, beginning with the prominently displayed letter *G* on the east wall (denoting *Geometry* and *God*), continuing through the elevated seat of the Worshipful Master (the presiding official), then the altar, and ending with the Senior Warden at the west wall. The secondary axis was perpendicular, passing through lesser officials and intersecting, again, at the altar.[4] The members sat along the four walls and faced the altar. Ritual activities commonly involved processions along the perimeter of the box defined by the seated membership. Just as members were taught to move their fingers, hands, and arms in precise, angular ways, they also proceeded through the ritual space of the temple in precise rectilinear and symmetrical patterns.

The geometrical and mathematical precision of the temple space is particularly striking when considered in relation to an analogous and equally important ritual space in Victorian America: the parlor. Visitors to both temple and parlor sought admission by presenting credentials (an application in the first instance, a calling card in the second) to a gatekeeper (a Tyler with a sword, a maid with a silver tray), who submitted it to the arbiter of the space (a lodge officer, the lady of the house). Doors opened and closed, and the ritual acquired dramatic power as visitors waited to see if they would be granted or denied entry and acceptance.

The visual iconography of the parlor was, however, antithetical to the rectilinear and abstract geometrical order of the Masonic space. In the parlor, wrote historian Thomas J. Schlereth, "clutter was class."[5] Families of even modest means transformed these rooms into congeries of ceramic trees and birds and interrupted the smooth planes of the walls with prints and pictures. Moldings and other forms of mass-produced ornamentation reiterated naturalistic themes and provided additional picturesque detail. Drapes and curtains, printed in leaf and flower patterns and suspended from windows, door frames, and moldings, further muted or "softened" the room's hard lines.

Count it certain that the Truth will always win and the right prevail in the end. The principal lesson "Teach Men how to be Free."

In *How to Furnish a Home* (1881), Ella Rodman Church explained that the parlor should evoke "lightness and beauty," with furniture that was "well-stuffed." Wood should be covered with soft fabrics, and where exposed, it was to exhibit "the least angularity." Chairs were to imitate the "natural curve" of the body. [6] In 1880 *Harper's Bazaar* commented on the transformation of interior space within the home since 1840, when the parlor had been characterized by "absolute simplicity"—or, the magazine added, with a gender-laden emphasis, "one might better say baldness." "But how have customs undergone a change into something rich and strange!" The modern parlor, though "a little overcrowded," was "crowded only with beauty." "What a desert was that old parlor to this!" [7] The dining room quickly became a visual adjunct of the parlor; from 1850 to 1870, as Kenneth Ames has observed, it was added to the parlor as "female territory." Gone was the "bold, strong, forceful, assertive, and aggressive" furniture that, in the Victorian mind, signified "masculine goods." [8]

The ritual space of the men's lodge—rectilinear, symmetrical, mathematically ordered—was the visual antithesis of the ritual space of the "feminized" parlor—profusely ornamented, naturalistic in detail, devoid of solid masses. Even today, Scottish Rite initiates recall feeling overwhelmed when blindfolds were removed and a dazzling light stunned dilated pupils. First they discerned familiar faces among the sea of men and then the ordered grandeur of the temple itself. Most recognized that they were inhabiting what may have been the most "masculine" space they had ever beheld.

The backdrop for the fourth degree (FIG. 5) conveyed masculinity in yet another way. The ritual emphasized the power of reason, of man's capacity to control and reorder the world around him, and the symmetrical lines and imposing masses of Solomon's temple demonstrated the power of geometry, a manifestation of human reason. The implicit theology of this arrangement suggested that God demonstrates his will indirectly through expressions of human intellect—most impressively through magnificent buildings. The Masonic god was impersonal, reclusive, an "All Seeing Eye" or "omnipresent Jehovah" who painstakingly concealed his name and essence. His will was synonymous with purist abstractions, such as mathematics (thus, the Scottish Rite fascination with magical numbers) and geometry.

### *Stridently Masculine Design and Decor*

Within the Masonic temple dwelt a deity of mathematical abstractions. By contrast, within another semisacred Victorian space, the home, Protestant women advanced a conception of a loving God, one who heard the softest voices of his kingdom and responded personally. Those who worshiped this "feminized," liberal God discerned his work in the soft radiance of a summer sunset or the delicacy of a flower, not in expressions of man's ambition, such as trains and cities, the brick and

*80*

FIGS · 7 & 8

A plan for layout of the grounds and an Illustrated
image of a small cottage. From Andrew Jackson
Downing, *Victorian Cottage Residences* (New York:
Dover, 1981; originally published 1842).

steel embodiments of economic and political power. As landscape architect Andrew Jackson Downing
explained in *Victorian Cottage Residences* (1842): "If we become sincere lovers of the grace, the harmony, and the loveliness with which rural homes and rural life are capable of being invested, we shall
attain a nearer view of the Great Master, whose words, in all his material universe, are written in lines
of Beauty." [9]

Downing conceived of these metaphysical "lines of Beauty" quite literally and believed
that particular home designs could express this religious view and impart meaning to the inhabitants.
To approximate nature's "lines of grace and softness," therefore, he eliminated "rigid lines and hard
mathematical angles"; to reduce the hubristic sense of man-made mass, he subdivided the house into a
cluster of small spatial units; to efface flat walls, he pierced planes with windows and bays and utilized
decorative planks to soften what remained unadorned; to blur the sharp roofline, he threw up a forest
of chimneys; to suggest that the house had grown organically from the earth, he concealed the foun-
dation behind a tangle of shrubbery; and to evoke a setting within nature, he insisted that pathways
and approach roads wander toward the house like a brook (FIGS. 7, 8).

English art critic John Ruskin advocated this aesthetic in *The Stones of Venice* (1849)
and *The Seven Lamps of Architecture* (1854), works that enjoyed great popularity among the American
middle classes. Ruskin argued against the "masculine" aesthetic found in the "abstract power and
awfulness" of flat planes, of straight lines, of the sheer drop of precipitous walls. True beauty emana-
ted instead from living nature, in which God's hand was perceptible. Thus, "forms which are not taken
from natural objects must be ugly"; conversely, "beautiful forms must be composed of curves," because
there were "hardly any common natural forms in which it is possible to discover a straight line." [10]

If Victorian homes in subsequent decades accorded with this feminized aesthetic,
Scottish Rite temples and especially the backdrops painted for the rituals were, in many instances, its

81

FIG·9

(top) The Sosman and Landis Studios created this "secret vault" in 1908; used in the fourteenth degree by the Scottish Rite temple in Wichita, Kansas. Courtesy of the Scottish Rite Bodies of Wichita, KS (See Brockman, Figs. 12 and 13.)

FIG·10

(bottom) This sketch, created by Sosman and Landis, represents the "rebuilding of the Temple." Courtesy of the Holak Collection, from the Performing Arts Archives of the University of Minnesota Libraries

Theatre of the Fraternity

visual antithesis. The rituals that took place in "secret vaults" within Solomon's temple (FIG. 9) were depicted with massive columns, unyieldingly symmetrical structures, ponderous masses, and threatening contrasts of light and shadow. Even the rituals that were set outdoors bore few traces of flora and fauna, and the backdrops for these repudiated the "feminized" aesthetic of Henry Ward Beecher, Ruskin, and Downing. For example, several rituals featured an exterior view of Solomon's temple (FIG. 10), but the accompanying scenery did not evoke a sweetly picturesque natural world. In the foreground loom the ruins of the temple, cluttered at the base with heavy stone blocks; the center of the temple—its lines clean, austere, and angular despite the ruination—is recessed toward the middle. In the distance, palm trees symbolize chaos, which gradually destroyed the serene order of the temple.

Nature did figure more explicitly in the backdrops of several other rituals, perhaps most obviously for the seventeenth degree. This long and complicated degree included scenes in which the initiate's head was "purified" with water and his arm pricked with a lancet as "proof of his fidelity and courage." The purpose of these rites was to affirm the initiate's worthiness to open the seven seals of the Great Book (FIG. 11). As he broke each seal, nature responded with spectacular effects: Hail and fire "mingled with blood" fell upon the earth; a great star dropped from the heavens; the sun, moon, and stars were eclipsed; demons flew out, inflicting "savage torture" and death upon mankind; finally, there were an earthquake and a "great mountain vomiting fire."

The scene illustrated what art historian Angela Miller calls the "strenuous masculine associations of the romantic mountain sublime" of mid-nineteenth-century landscape painters such as Thomas Cole, whose vast panoramas overwhelm the observer. Eventually, this masculine representation of nature fell into disfavor. The prescient Ruskin best described the religious forces accounting for the shift: "God is not in the earthquake, nor in the fire, but in the still small voice."[11] In 1855 Henry Ward Beecher contended that tranquil woodland scenes were preferable to "august mountains, wide panoramas, awful gorges . . . any thing that runs in upon you with strong stimulations."[12] Five years later, Thomas Starr King dismissed as "mere appetite" the landscape painters' earlier attraction to "wildness, ruggedness, and the feeling of mass and precipitous elevation," images that inevitably gave way to "the refined grandeur, the chaste sublimity, the airy majesty overlaid with tender and polished bloom, in which the landscape splendor of a noble mountain lies." Painters such as Jasper Cropsey, Sanford Gifford, and others "softened," in Miller's words, the "assertive shapes and masses" of mountains with "atmospheric veils."[13]

But while the most important artists in the Gilded Age were moving toward a more subtle rendering of landscapes, those with a popular following often emulated the "strong stimulations" achieved by painters such as Cole. The painted backdrops for the Scottish Rite in the 1890s, which evoked the masculine sublime of the 1840s and 1850s, exemplify this approach. The cave of the

83

ninth degree is typical of this view of nature, which is represented in other backdrops as well. For example, those of the third and ninth degrees (FIG. 13), which provide a setting for the "raising" of the murdered Hiram Abiff, contained pronounced elements of the masculine sublime. Nearly all these show a mountain, or large hill, rising precipitously from the cave, often with massive boulders in the foreground and craggy peaks in the distance; in some, the cave is replaced with a mausoleum with sharply articulated rectilinear blocks. The backdrops for many other degrees show a preference for symmetrical, rectilinear interiors with smooth planes and great mass and for imposingly grand evocations of natural phenomena.

### Temporizing Effects of Feminism

Thus, as members of the Scottish Rite left their homes and entered the Masonic temple, they moved from a space whose visual elements murmured "femininity" to one where those elements declared "masculinity." The Scottish Rite temple was a ritual space for men only, and its design and decor reinforced that fact. Although many Masonic lodges did admit women for special events, they were never allowed to witness the initiations of their menfolk. [14]

Visually and aesthetically, the Scottish Rite temple was wondrously complex. The Philadelphia temple, for instance, contained seven lodge rooms, each with detailed elaborations of dramatically different interiors and icons, ranging from a medieval great hall to an Egyptian mausoleum. (See Moore, FIGS. 6 & 7.) In addition to variations among the thousands of lodges, each degree required its own paraphernalia, costumes, and backdrops, so it is impossible to describe in general terms the appearance of Victorian Masonic lodges. Furthermore, while the masculine aesthetic generally prevailed in the lodges, and particularly in the painted backdrops of the Scottish Rite, there are several significant instances where this aesthetic was tempered with feminine imagery.

The most obvious example was the costumes members wore for initiation ceremonies. Although Scottish Rite Masons adorned themselves with angular shapes and squares and moved in prescribed rectilinear patterns, they also wore gowns and aprons, often decorated with ribbons, lace, and fringe. Material-culture expert Barbara Franco, struck by the "delicacy," the "surprisingly feminine" character of Masonic artifacts, cites a mid-nineteenth-century critic of the orders who described fraternal members as "he-woman wearers of ribbons, and shot aprons and tin jewels." [15]

And while the backdrops of most Scottish Rite degrees were insistently masculine in character, some plainly were not. In the nineteenth and thirty-second degree, the Gothic cathedral— in some lodges, an Indian temple—was intensely ornamented, with no planar surfaces and little sense of mass (FIGS. 14, 15). Scenery for the thirty-second, and final, degree showed countless reiterations of curved tents: again, no mass, no surface planes, no straight lines (FIG. 16). And the backdrop for the

FIG·12

This backdrop with foliage cut drop was created from the sketch (fig. 11) in 1952 for the Scottish Rite temple in Kansas City, Kansas. Courtesy of the Scottish Rite Bodies of Kansas City, KS

22ND DEGREE • KNIGHT OF THE ROYAL AXE

FIG·13

This backdrop depicting a cave with waterfalls was created by the Sosman and Landis Studios in 1908 for the Scottish Rite temple in Wichita, Kansas. This drop can be used in both the ninth degree of the Scottish Rite and the third degree of the Blue Lodge. Courtesy of the Scottish Rite Bodies of Wichita, KS

Teaches the dignity of Labor, that it is not a curse, but a privilege for man to earn his sustenance by work.

fifteenth degree, with a tracery of foliage in the foreground, showed a stream flowing sinuously through a sequence of rolling hills, an idyllic setting for the picturesque cottage such as Andrew Jackson Downing had proposed as an expression of feminine domesticity. (See Clawson, FIG. 8.)

This juxtaposition of masculine and feminine aesthetics appears most strikingly in the backdrop for the eighteenth degree, Knight Rose Croix. Because this ritual was the culminating degree for the first half of Scottish Rite Freemasonry, even lodges that could not afford to stage all the degrees made an effort to do this one as elaborately as possible. Even today, Masons speak of it as one of the most memorable rituals. Long, complex, and elaborate, it required at least three separate rooms or backdrops. The initiate traveled in search of the "sacred word," with different backdrops illustrating his progress—from a darkened Chamber of Reflection, complete with skull and Bible, to the hill of Calvary, and finally, to the wastes of Hell, where hideous figures devoured naked human beings and serpents writhed among skeletons.

The masculine elements of the degree were obvious: grotesque representations of Hell, the glowing skull in the all-black Chamber of Reflection, the gruesome oath of secrecy ("my blood continually running from my body"),[16] and the repeated allusions to angular geometric figures, especially a "cubic stone that sweats blood." Yet the feminine elements were nearly as pronounced. For instance, initiates were obliged to produce "women's gloves" as gifts to spouses and to wear "veils" (the blindfold) and ribbons with jewels; most striking were the explicit references to Christ, who had become the chief symbol and exemplar for the "feminized" Protestantism of Victorian America.

The backdrop for this ritual (FIG. 17) reflects this juxtaposition of masculine and feminine themes. On the right-hand side are traditionally masculine symbols. Massive boulders tumbling from a jagged cliff uproot straight trees, whose dead limbs scratch across the angular columns; a stream rages down the mountain, upon which is perched an eagle searching for prey. But iconography on the left-hand side evokes an entirely different mood. A distant haze softens the mountains; the stream winds sinuously through a lush plain covered with flowers on all sides; a pelican, the symbol of Christ, pricks its breast to let her young drink her blood (FIG. 19); and pink roses delicately curl around the column, a stock image of a traditionally feminine Victorian garden party.

The fact that the backdrop depicted stereotypical visual elements of both masculine and feminine gender aesthetics raises several questions. Why, for instance, did men in the lodge wear gowns, ribbons, and veils with feminine connotations if they went there to escape the feminine domesticity of the home? If they longed to perform initiatory rites to confirm a sense of masculinity, why did they do so in some environments rife with feminine imagery?

86

FIG · 14

(top) The Great Western Stage Equipment Company created this sketch for the Gothic cathedral used in the nineteenth degree. Courtesy of the Great Western Stage Equipment Collection from the Performing Arts Archives of the University of Minnesota Libraries

FIG · 15

(bottom) The Volland Scenic Studios created this sketch for the cathedral scene, also used in the thirty-second degree. Together with the sketch in fig. 14, it demonstrates the variation of style and artistic choices available. Courtesy of C. Michael Volland, Volland Scenic Studios, St. Louis, MO

87

Scottish Rite and the Visual Semiotics of Gender

FIG · 16

The Sosman and Landis Studios created this colored sketch for the encampment scene of the thirty-second degree. Courtesy of the Holak Collection from the Performing Arts Archives of the University of Minnesota Libraries

FIG · 17

The Sosman and Landis Studios created this colored sketch for a backdrop and cut drop for the peristyle scene of the eighteenth degree. Courtesy of the Holak Collection from the Performing Arts Archives of the University of Minnesota Libraries

24TH DEGREE · PRINCE OF THE TABERNACLE

No man hath power over the spirit; neither power in the day of death.

FIG · 18

This backdrop was created from the sketch in fig. 17 and painted for the Scottish Rite temple in Wichita, Kansas, in 1908. Courtesy of the Scottish Rite Bodies of Wichita, KS

FIG · 19
Detail of pelican feeding her young from fig. 17.

### Gender Elements Juxtaposed

The historical record is silent on these difficult questions. Scottish Rite Masons did not discuss rituals they had sworn to keep secret, and even if they did, most would have been hard-pressed to explain what the ceremonies meant to them. My answers are, therefore, necessarily speculative and turn on one salient point: women's complete and absolute absence from men's Scottish Rite initiations. Their exclusion was so obvious that no one felt compelled even to refer to it. The universal acceptance of this pointed exclusion of women was an essential feature of Masonic initiations.

It seems reasonable to surmise that women were excluded from the lodge because men wanted to immerse themselves in a masculine setting, which in Victorian America meant one that enshrined the power of reason (geometry, for instance, or its applications through engineering and technology), the wholesome uses of aggression (defeating enemies and overcoming fears), and the value of patriarchy (respect for forebears and the institutions they devised). In the lodge rooms of the Scottish Rite, men "worshiped" icons that symbolized, in Victorian America, these masculine traits.

Yet the message of the rituals, and of Masonic material culture, further suggests a duality: While Victorian men were attracted to an idealized masculinity, they also found it oppressive. They wearied of the ceaseless struggles with unseen enemies, especially in the raucously competitive world of late-nineteenth-century capitalism. They sometimes tired as well of the need to appear strong and, at home, to assume the role of the always rational, dispassionate patriarch. Although this role granted the player many privileges and sources of satisfaction and power, it also dictated and constrained certain thoughts and behaviors.

The popularity of Louisa May Alcott's Jo in *Little Women* and of other strong-minded, independent heroines in Victorian literature attests to the ambivalence many Victorian women felt toward the corseted role they were expected to play—that of self-effacing paragons of maternal solicitude and Christian piety. Victorian America had imposed upon adult women a prescribed set of behaviors that narrowly defined their emotions and actions. How such women subtly wrested emotional sustenance from the obdurate limitations of their roles has been a central theme in recent women's history.

The popularity of fraternal rituals indicates that many men similarly longed to experience more latitude in their emotional lives than accorded with the public perception of Victorian males. On lodge nights, men who had climbed the corporate ladder, their every step painstakingly modulated to appease and impress bosses, exulted in the explicit challenges and confrontations, the bloody oaths and quests for vengeance, the swords, the crowns, and the mitres of authority. When the lights blazed forth and the men strode across the stage, they wielded power: They bound up and "tortured" initiates; they searched for and punished evildoers; they promulgated laws and moral codes.

89

**Its image lifted on high, kneels and restores to life. Here we learn the mysteries of creation.**

Tobacconists became kings, and clerks, ancient patriarchs. Here men who aspired to the idealized roles of Victorian masculinity found what had proved to be so elusive outside the lodge.

But because they were so obviously acting a role—their identities further obscured by blindfolds, costumes, beards, and masks—these same men also assumed nurturing and sentimental behaviors that, in Victorian America, were strongly associated with women. If they sometimes played the role of king or executioner, they also, as initiates for the degrees, consented to being bound up, blindfolded, tugged around the lodge, and otherwise "humiliated." In some rituals they comforted the sick, and in others they submitted to the authority of "elders." But in every ritual they transformed the lodge into an affective family, embracing "brothers" and comforting "sons," all the while uttering sentimental pieties about the need for "submission, humility, and industry." Freemasonry, it seemed, was ultimately feminine, and members invariably identified it with the feminine pronouns.

But these behaviors—both the hyper-masculine and hyper-feminine ones—could be indulged only within the ritualized, theatrical context of the lodge room. The darkness, the costumes, the prescribed lines, and the backdrops all reinforced the complex gender messages of the rituals. No wonder secrecy was essential. If, say, an insurance salesman demanded deference at the office, he would be thought mad; if he waved a sword, he would be put away; if he allowed other men to tie him up and embrace him, he would be regarded as unmanly and otherwise unfit. But within the magical, secret realm of the lodge, that man—and thousands like him—could express thoughts and perform actions that would have been entirely inappropriate elsewhere.

The temples, lodge rooms, scenery, and costumes of the Scottish Rite were revealing expressions of the material culture of Victorian America, bearing as they did the distinctive markings of that era's technology, economic system, and social relations. And the Rite's ambiguous visual gender code not only reflected Victorian life, but it also provided members with a complex and subtle way to strike an emotionally satisfying balance between their masculine and feminine natures.

*90*

*1* Albert Pike, comp., *Morals and Dogma of Freemasonry* (Charleston: Southern Jurisdiction, A.A.S.R., 1871), 106.

*2* Fraternal rituals were mostly an oral tradition, passed down according to the usages and traditions of millions of different participants and thousands of different lodges; these usages have changed substantially since the late nineteenth century. The accounts of Scottish Rite degrees described here are from the following nineteenth-century sources: Jonathan Blanchard, comp., *Scotch Rite Masonry Illustrated* (Chicago: Ezra Cook, 1882), and Albert Pike, *The Magnum Opus, or Great Work* (Kila, MT: Kessinger, 1992).

*3* See Roosevelt's article, "Manliness and Decency," from *Men* 22, no. 39 (Feb. 6, 1897), as cited in Clifford Putney, "Muscular Christianity: The Strenuous Mood in American Protestantism: 1880–1920" (unpublished Ph.D diss., Brandeis University, 1994).

*4* William D. Moore, "The Masonic Lodge Room, 1870–1930: A Sacred Space of Masculine Spiritual Hierarchy," in *Gender, Class, and Shelter: Perspectives in Vernacular Architecture*, vol. 5, Elizabeth Collins Cromley and Carter L. Hudgins, eds. (Knoxville: University of Tennessee Press, 1995).

*5* Thomas J. Schlereth, *Victorian America: Transformations in Everyday Life* (New York: Harper Collins, 1991), 117; Harvey Wish, *The Light of the Home: An Intimate View of the Lives of Women in Victorian America* (New York: Pantheon, 1986), 101.

*6* Ella Rodman Church, *How to Furnish a Home* (Boston: E.P. Putnam, 1881), 207.

*7* "Forty Years Ago, and Now," *Harper's Bazaar* 13, no. 33 (Aug. 14, 1880).

*8* Kenneth L. Ames, *Death in the Dining Room and Other Tales of Victorian Culture* (Philadelphia: Temple University Press, 1992), 74, 93.

*9* Andrew Jackson Downing, *Victorian Cottage Residences* (New York: Dover, 1981; originally published 1842).

*10* John Ruskin, *The Seven Lamps of Architecture* (New York: Dover, 1989; originally published 1880), 77, 105, 108.

*11* *Modern Painters: The Works of John Ruskin*, E.T. Cook and Alexander Wedderburn, eds. (London: George Allen, 1903), 3:345.

*12* Henry Ward Beecher, *Star Papers; or, Experiences of Art and Nature* (New York: J. C. Derby, 1855), 308, cited in Angela Miller, *Empire of the Eye* (Ithaca: Cornell University Press, 1992), 252.

*13* Miller, 257.

*14* On women's support for Masonic fundraising, see William D. Moore, "Funding the Temples of Masculinity: Women's Roles in Masonic Fairs in New York State, 1870–1930," *Nineteenth Century* 14, no. 1 (1994).

*15* Barbara Franco, in *Theatre of the Fraternity: Staging the Space of the Scottish Rite*, C. Lance Brockman, ed. With respect to aprons, William D. Moore observed that many male artisans—bakers, blacksmiths, and stonemasons—wore such aprons. He added that by the late nineteenth century, Masonic aprons were plainer and made of sturdier material (personal communication with author).

*16* The quote is from the draft version of Pike's *Magnum Opus*. S. Brent Morris informs me that all physical penalties were dropped when the final version of the rituals was adopted (personal communication with author).

*91*

# THEATRE AND THE FRATERNITY

CREATING SCENIC ILLUSION FOR THE

**C. LANCE BROCKMAN**

Thomas Gibbs Moses was a leading scenic artist, who, during his sixty-year career, created backgrounds for major actors and producers, including Joseph Jefferson, Madame Mojeska, and the Ringling Brothers. In addition, Moses painted and designed scenery for more than fifty-five Scottish Rite temples and seven Shrine mosques. His unpublished diary, excerpts of which are quoted in this essay, chronicles the life of one of America's most prolific scenic artists and provides an unusual insight into both the theatre and the fraternity.

The scene-painter is like a doctor; he is called in either to build up the constitution of a robust drama or to save a weak one from sudden death. It is admitted that, in the case of a poor play, the more attractive the scenic illusions the better the chances of success, and therefore, in the case of the play owing its prosperity to its being a picture gallery, there can be manifestly no conventional limit to the artistic excellence which may be put in it. [1]

L ATE-NINETEENTH-CENTURY AMERICAN AUDIENCES POSSESSED AN INSATIABLE APPETITE FOR THE ILLUSIONARY CREATIONS OF THEATRICAL SCENIC ARTISTS. The public flocked to local opera houses and theatres not to see the restaging of all-too-familiar plays but to experience the "greatest logjam ever staged," the "eruption of Mount Vesuvius," or "the great train wreck." The dramatization of popular novels such as *Around the World in Eighty Days*, *20,000 Leagues Under the Sea*, and *Ben Hur: A Tale of the Christ* provided incredible opportunities for these scenic artists to create imaginary, romanticized worlds that transformed the stage (FIG. 1).

**1892** *I made models for* Ben-Hur. *I enjoyed this work — very interesting. This was before the story was dramatized. It was to be done in tableaux and pantomine* [sic].

Besides creating scenic backgrounds for the commercial stage, many theatre artists also painted illusionary worlds for other late-Victorian entertainments such as historic panoramas, fairs, and expositions (FIGS. 2, 3), stages for ethnic halls (FIG. 4), and amusement parks. Their stylized interpretations of the world recalled, in the words of late-nine-teenth-century artist Edward Burne-Jones, "a beautiful romantic dream of something that never was . . . in a land no one can define or remember, only desire." [2] In order to meet the demand for this variety of magical worlds, these scenic artists had to possess a visual dexterity aptly described in a 1900 article titled "Stage Scenery and the Men Who Paint It":

In fact, a scene painter must be a cyclopedia of architectural styles. Persia, Greece, Rome, Ireland and Siberia, Italian gardens and the western plains must all be at his command. He must know periods and epochs, he must be an authority in matters of appropriate decoration and ornament, for there is no time now for research [3] (FIGS. 2–6).

FIG · 2

A Javenese village for the Midway Plaissance
of the Columbian Exposition, Chicago, 1893. The
Sosman and Landis Scene Painting Studios
created the backdrop and interior decoration.
From Hubert Howe Bancroft, *The Book
of the Fair* (Chicago: The Bancroft Co., 1893).

FIG · 3

Sosman and Landis used this sketch to create
the volcano backdrop for the seventeenth degree
of the Scottish Rite. See Lawrence Hill's essay
for a full description of the lighting effects used
during the ritual. Courtesy of the Holak
Collection, from the Performing Arts Archives of
the University of Minnesota Libraries

FIG · 4

This front, or drop, curtain with a view of Prague,
Czechoslovakia, was painted by Sosman and
Landis for an ethnic hall in Oxford Junction, Iowa.
Courtesy of the Museum of Repertoire
Americana, Mt. Pleasant, IA

FIG · 5
Act III, Tableau 1, "Room in the House of
Simonides in Antioch" from *Ben Hur: the Souvenir
Album—Scenes of the Play*, produced by
Klaw and Erlanger, 1900. Courtesy of the author

FIG · 6
A backdrop and cut drop painted by the Sosman
and Landis Studios and used for Solomon's
apartment in the sixth degree of the Scottish Rite.
Courtesy of the Scottish Rite Bodies, Salina, KS

95

The first theatre illusionists in this country were itinerant artists with varying levels of skill who followed the westward expansion. The more talented painters were employed by opera houses in established eastern cities; others pushed west, painting and decorating the interiors of public and private buildings, as well as scenic backgrounds for the opera houses, theatres, and stages of ethnic halls found in every town, large and small, across the country.

Theatres required a "stock" system of scenery that provided a generic set of locations, such as a rocky mountain pass, a deep woods (FIGS. 7–9), a Gothic interior, a palace, a garden, a decorative drop curtain (FIGS. 10, 11), and so on. This scenery consisted of two distinct parts: backdrops and cut drops, or wings. The backdrops were the central composition, the basic subject matter of the scene, and traditionally were painted on expanses of cotton muslin, or "for large scenery and special sets," on Russian linen.[4] Surrounding the backdrops were cut drops painted to resemble generic trees, rocks, or interior walls; the cut pieces completed the visual edges of the composition while masking or covering the offstage areas. When painted on fabric that was stretched over wooden frames, these cut pieces were called wings. When combined the result was called wing-and-drop scenery (FIGS. 12, 13).

> **1 9 1 3**  *I completed in less than eight hours, a dark wood drop, 24 x 40, without help. That is something I never accomplished before—that much in that time. Sosman was pleased with it. I didn't wait for anything to dry—worked in the wet.*

The economic resources of the theatre, opera house, or ethnic hall determined the amount of scenery installed. According to a 1889 scenic catalog, the most complete installation contained more than a hundred pieces "comprising about all that will ever be called for, with the exception of 'A Special Production.'" For theatres with limited resources, the variety of visual locales could be reduced from thirty-seven to only eighteen pieces that "will suit an ordinary Hall very nicely."[5]

By the 1880s, railroads connected the American coasts and effectively ended both local control of the professional opera houses and theatres while altering the commercial practices of the burgeoning numbers of scenic artists. Theatre became a centralized business with national authority. As a result, productions were mounted "more with a view to road tour profits than for their artistic success."[6] The itinerant artists were squeezed out by the "studio system," which used the railroad network to move the product to the consumer. The emerging scenic studios employed only the best artists, hiring a complement of genre or specialty painters who were "selected for their particular skill and ability in their different lines of work. Some do Drop Curtain work exclusively; others Exterior Scenes; still others Interiors, Draperies, etc., etc. By this method our patrons get the highest skill of a number of artists in their work, and the result is better work than any individual could do."[7]

### The Beginnings: Theatre and the Fraternity

The omnivorous quest of scenic studios for additional commercial opportunities at the end of the nineteenth century fostered their close association with fraternal organizations. Superficially, the intersection of popular entertainment and theatre with the Scottish Rite of Freemasonry might seem coincidental, but a closer examination clearly indicates how the integration of scenery and lighting into this fraternity's ritual both heightened the initiation experience and increased business opportunities for the studios. For the fraternity, the addition of scenery, lighting, and stage effects made it possible to "mass produce" members and, as it did for turn-of-the-century theatres, to attract an ever-increasing membership, or audience.

Scenery was first used on the fraternal stage in Chicago in 1884. In a renovation of the "traditional" lodge space for the Scottish Rite, a stage was erected with "new scenery and properties, and all the paraphernalia for displaying panoramic scenes, with a handsome illustrated drop curtain and rich drapery in front"[8] (FIG. 14). The credit for "preparing and mounting" the scenery and stage effects was given to Prince J. S. (Joseph Sands) Sosman, a thirty-second-degree Mason and a partner in the Sosman and Landis Scene Painting Studios established in Chicago in 1875.[9]

By 1893 the various Masonic bodies in Chicago had outgrown their 1884 fraternal spaces and moved into a new temple heralded as the "tallest building in the world" (FIGS. 15, 16). This edifice was erected in the center of the business district and was hurriedly completed for the opening of the Columbian Exposition in order to host "Scottish Rite visitors from all parts of the world."[10] To the delight of the brethren, this demonstrated both a radical departure from past practices and the full potential of stage paraphernalia to "improve" the ritual degrees. In the eastern United States, the addition of a stage was, at first, impractical because most Masonic temples were built on the model of a traditional fraternal hall, with lodge rooms over commercial businesses. In developing parts of America, however, it was economically feasible to build a fully equipped theatre, and the result was a strange hybrid of amateur dramatics supported by state-of-the-art stagecraft.

> **1893** *The big Fair progressing nicely and a world of work for us in sight . . . We had a great many exhibits to do at the Fair and many outside shows . . . Shows like the "The Outsider," "Columbus" for Leavitt, "Fabio Romona," "The Black Crook," "A Day in the Swiss Alps," "South Sea Islanders." "Kansas State Exhibit," "The Laplanders," "Streets of Cairo," Javanese Theatre, Chinese Theatre, a dozen big floats, "Lady of Venice" for Buffalo Bill (W. F. Cody) and many others.*

### Little Rock, Wichita, and Guthrie

In 1896 the fledgling members of the Scottish Rite in Little Rock, Arkansas, under the leadership of Charles E. Rosenbaum, converted a synagogue into a stage space and equipped it with scenery from the Sosman and Landis Scene Painting Studios of Chicago (FIGS. 20, 21). The venture

FIGS · 12 & 13
The cut drop was a scenic device that framed the backdrops and completed the stage composition. Changing location in both the fraternal and popular stage was achieved by reusing the more generic cut drops in front of various backdrops. In this example, cut drops painted to resemble a rough stone arch frame both the secret vault of the fourteenth degree (fig. 13) and the catacombs used in the twenty-sixth degree (fig. 12). Courtesy of the John R. Rothgeb Papers, Theatre Arts Collection, Harry Ransom Humanities Research Center, University of Texas, Austin

FIG · 14
Interior view of the first Masonic stage installed in Chicago, in 1884. From Robert G. Cole, based on the writings of Gil. W. Barnard, "Ancient and Accepted Scottish Rite Valley of Chicago 1857–1957," *Chicago Scottish Rite Magazine* (April 1957).

FIG · 15
The Scottish Rite auditorium in the 1893 Chicago Masonic temple. From the thirty-eighth reunion program of the Oriental Consistory, Chicago. (See Moore, Fig. 14.) Courtesy of the Chancellor Robert R. Livingston Library and Museum of the Grand Lodge of New York

FIG·16

(above) Comparison of the Chicago Masonic temple, "the highest commercial building in the world," with Trinity Church, New York; the Statue of Liberty; the Capitol, Washington D. C.; and the Ferris wheel, the most identifiable symbol of the Columbian Exposition, 1893. "A City Under One Roof—The Masonic Temple," *Scientific American* (Feb. 10, 1894).

FIG·17

Sosman and Landis of Chicago provided the scenery that was installed on the first Masonic stage in the Southern Jursidiction in Little Rock, Arkansas, in 1896. From the *Fall Reunion Program* (Little Rock: Oct. 8–10, 1899) and archival papers. Courtesy of the Albert Pike Memorial Temple, Little Rock, AR

FIG·18

Charles E. Rosenbaum in the costume of the Master of Kadosh. From the *Fall Reunion Program* (Little Rock: Oct. 8–10, 1899). Courtesy of the Albert Pike Memorial Temple, Little Rock, AR

*101*

FIG·19

was immediately successful, and in 1898 further investment was made. The positive results were recorded as follows in a reunion program:

> The building has the same appearance outside as when you saw it last, but when you enter the auditorium, don't beat a retreat—thinking you are in the wrong place—it may take you a moment or two to become accustomed to the great change in the interior, but you will soon feel at home again, and will enjoy to a much greater extent the exemplification of the various degrees, assisted so materially by additional scenic and electrical effects, on which neither labor or expense have been spared, to the end that it might be the most perfect to produce.[11]

The Little Rock example was quickly mimicked in Wichita, Kansas, where in 1898 "the [Scottish Rite] Bodies bought the Y.M.C.A. building and after remodeling it to include stage, scenery, and auditorium, with seating capacity of about 300, the Wichita Consistory had a Temple of which it was duly proud and worth fully $100,000 with a comparatively small mortgage indebtedness"[12] (FIG 21). In 1900 Bestor G.(Gaston) Brown, the western representative for the large fraternal supplier M.C. Lilley Company, a Scottish Rite Mason from Wichita, and a stage director of the degrees, persuaded the brethren in Guthrie, Oklahoma, to build an auditorium equipped with "the needed scenery and other paraphernalia to properly dramatize the degrees"[13] (FIG. 23). Before acquiring a stage with theatre equipment, the Guthrie Scottish Rite Masons had made "their own paraphernalia, regalia, etc. [consisting of]—robes and draperies from black, red and white calico, an altar made from dry goods boxes, covered with the same black calico, upon which Barnes (a local sign painter) painted the required tear drops, transparencies fashioned from cigar boxes with tallow candles for the symbolic lights—all very crude and furnishing much amusement to the York Rite and Blue Lodge brethren, whose revenues permitted more elaborate regalia."[14]

By 1901 the change in the degree conferral from the floor of the lodge room to a stage in an auditorium was an accomplished fact.[15] Scottish Rite bodies across the country quickly emulated this new means of initiation. But at these three temples it presented some risk. For the brethren in Little Rock, Wichita, and Guthrie, this new initiation practice was done without national sanction and by "a method that was considered by other Supreme Councils of the World and by practically all of the older and more conservative Orients of our own Southern Jurisdiction as decidedly unethical— and if a word can be applied to Masonic work—as almost sacrilegious."[16]

Nonetheless, the success and popularity of including scenery, lighting, and visual effects at these three locations were irrefutable. By 1902, again under the leadership of Rosenbaum, Little Rock Masons built the first temple exclusively for the Scottish Rite; it was christened "the Gem

FIG · 20
Detail of the baldachin, or canopy, from the Solomon backdrop in fig. 19.

FIG · 22
Scenery for Solomon's temple as installed in 1922 by Sosman and Landis. Comparison of this scenery with that pictured in figs. 19–21 reveals the style shifts that occurred in the move to modernism.

FIG · 21
Color image of the original scenery from Wichita that was reinstalled in the Masonic temple at Yankton, South Dakota, 1910. Courtesy of the Yankton Scottish Rite Bodies

FIG · 23
Bestor G. (Gaston) Brown, the western representative for M. C. Lilley of Columbus, Ohio, and a thirty-second-degree Mason. Brown, the first stage director for the Scottish Rite, "assisted" new temples in assimilating the scenery, costumes, and lighting on arrival. From the 1901 Centennial Reunion Program. Courtesy of the Scottish Rite Bodies, Wichita, KS

FIG · 24
A sketch from the Toomey and Volland Scenic Studio created for Solomon's temple (sixth degree) and installed in the St. Louis Scottish Rite temple in 1902. Courtesy of C. Michael Volland, Volland Scenic Studios, St. Louis, MO

**1925**  *The Scottish-Rite Bodies (of Pasadena) are well pleased with the layout that we have arranged for their new stage, using the old scenery from Little Rock, Arkansas, which I took in part payment when I put in the new equipment at the Albert Pike Memorial for Chas. E. Rosenbaum.*

of the Southern Jurisdiction."[17] Six years later the Wichita brethren added a larger auditorium to its Masonic building, "believing that the Scottish Rite Degrees had greater possibilities for more elaborate dramatization." According to a history of the Wichita Scottish Rite, a committee including Brown and Rosenbaum collaborated with scenic artists and costume manufacturers to develop the full theatrical potential "for stage effects."[18] By 1923 the new $3 million Scottish Rite temple in Guthrie was built on the four-block site of the old Capitol Square. With its two theatre spaces, the building is arguably one of the most elaborate and ambitious fraternal structures in the country.[19]

### Scenery for the Fraternity

At the turn of the century, the variety of locations and historical epochs required to support the Scottish Rite initiation was well within the visual vocabulary of the scenic artists who created fantasy worlds for all forms of popular entertainment (FIG. 21). Theatre plays such as *Egyptia, Athenian, Quo Vadis, Judas, Ben Hur,* and *King Solomon,* produced for Ringling Brothers' Circus in 1914, provided specific opportunities for this legion of artists to create exotic worlds that easily adapted to the fraternal stage.[20] Thomas Moses, the leading scenic artist for Sosman and Landis, recorded in his diary in 1909 that "the Masonic work requires a lot of time, and there is an average of eighty drops in each order so it makes plenty of work and it is very interesting. The artists never grumble when they get to do it."[21]

Following the early lead of Sosman and Landis, the Toomey and Volland Studio in St. Louis began to seek fraternal business in 1902 (FIGS. 24, 26–28). Other companies including Kansas City Scenic, the Twin City [Minneapolis/St. Paul] Scenic Studio, the Tiffin [Ohio] Studio, and the Great Western Stage Equipment Company of Kansas City soon did likewise.[22]

With the new century, the style of stage scenery began to evolve from a Victorian romanticized realism to a more "modern" graphic abstraction. In a 1921 article in *Billboard* titled "The Stage—Scenically," a theatre manager characterized these contrasting aesthetics: "It has been my casual observation that the scenic artist of yesterday appealed to the sense of realism and succeeded admirably, while the scenic artist of today strives to please the eye with a harmony of color and design rather than being geometrically perfect, and they, too, are succeeding admirably."[23] But for scenic artists trained in the late-nineteenth-century tradition, the emerging style was suspect. Many felt betrayed by

**1925**  *On the 28th I was a 32nd Degree Mason and very proud and thankful for it. It was like a dream to me and all my Masonic knowledge was only padded over by the ritual and some new work which was thankfully received. So after forty years of designing and painting these degrees, I will now go into the work with a much better understanding.*

Times change and circumstances, but virtue and duty remain the same. The True Knight prefers death to the abandonment of the post of duty.

(top) Thomas G. Moses created this sketch
of scenery for Darius's palace (16th degree) for
Sosman and Landis in the late 1920s or early
1930s. Compare this image with fig. 21 for changes
in scenic styles resulting from improvements
in lighting and the influence of more "modern"
graphic styles. Courtesy of the John R. Rothgeb
Papers, Theatre Arts Collection, Harry Ransom
Humanities Research Center, University
of Texas, Austin

F I G · 2 6

(bottom) Scenery created from the sketch
for the Scottish Rite Bodies of Richmond, Virginia,
and installed in 1920. Courtesy of the Richmond
Scottish Rite Bodies

106

FIG · 27

A detail of a distant tower from the
scenery pictured in fig. 26. Courtesy of the
Richmond Scottish Rite Bodies

Teaches that all men might be free, but ignorance and superstition forge the letters, and men enchain themselves and create their own bondage.

the replacement of Victorian "prettiness" with a visual milieu that reflected the vast and sometimes alarming changes in the emerging American culture. As the author in the *Billboard* article wrote, "The present trend of scenery is for simplicity. This is not surprising when you stop to think what a change the interior decorations of our home have undergone, to say nothing of a much simpler architecture."[24]

By the late 1920s, the demand for painted romantic realism was minimal, and the scenic painter found fewer outlets for his diverse talents. As early as 1923, Moses had articulated the plight of the few remaining artists: "Very little painted scenery for the vaudeville acts is being done, mostly fabrics, and if the wage scale keeps on, I don't see where the artists are going to find enough painting. They will have to become dress makers and learn to sew on sateens and velours. A few of the old melodramas would be very welcomed."[25]

The fraternal stage continued to provide for the older artists the melodramatic form that necessitated the creation of a late-nineteenth-century view of the world. By 1905 the Shrine, Grotto, and other Masonic bodies produced additional opportunities for the remaining scenic studios, but it was the Scottish Rite, with its complex degrees and rich mid-nineteenth-century text, that provided the most lucrative opportunity to apply a vanishing aesthetic. The traditional, romantically painted wings and backdrops that had delighted American audiences from the earliest colonial days were gradually being relegated to the musical and opera and to high-school stages. In their place was more sculptural and abstract scenery.

By 1929 the business of both the theatre and the fraternity changed drastically. Most

107

of the hundreds of scenic studios that had thrived on popular entertainment from the 1880s on went out of business. The scenic artists "just couldn't disappear and had to become free lancers . . . As the economy slowly improved—work was to be had on Industrial exhibits, Home shows and Auto shows etc."[26] Ironically, the remaining scene painters returned to the itinerant life that their predecessors had led before the heyday of the scenic studio.

Even the Scottish Rite of Freemasonry had, by 1930, ceased building many temples with fraternal stages. Although the drama and ritual that exist today are similar in form and content to the mid-nineteenth-century version of the degrees as rewritten by Albert Pike, the addition of full scenic backgrounds and lighting effects at the end of the century took the fraternity in a different direction than the founders originally intended. It moved from a mid-Victorian oral tradition to a visual interpretation of the "world of the ritual" that was consistent with late-nineteenth-century popular entertainment. By incorporating the accoutrements of the professional stage in its initiation ceremonies, the fraternity was able to survive and prosper into the twentieth century (FIG. 28). The fact that much of the early-twentieth-century Scottish Rite material culture still exists gives scholars and the public a glimpse into a bygone world. The settings, props, and lighting contained in these temples represent a time capsule that illuminates an intriguing period for both the theatre and the fraternity.

**1 9 3 0**  From a letter Thomas G. Moses wrote to Frank Jefferson of Little Rock, Arkansas: *I don't know how to thank you enough for the wonderful portrait you have been kind enough to send me. I will now have the 3 men that had all to do with the starting of the scenic decoration of the Scottish Rite Degree work—[Charles E.] Rosenbaum, [Bestor Gaston] Brown and [Joseph Sands] Sosman.*

[1] Richard Martson, "Art in the Theatre: The Decline of Scenic Art in America," *The Magazine of Art* 17 (1894), 164.

[2] Quoted in Ida Proctor, *Masters of British Nineteenth Century Art* (London: Dennis Dobson, 1961), 157.

[3] Mary Gay Humphreys, "Stage Scenery and the Men Who Paint It," *The Theatre Magazine* (1900), p.v.

[4] Catalog, *Sosman and Landis Scence Painting Studios: Scenery for Theatres, Opera Houses and Halls* (Chicago: 1889), n.p.

[5] Ibid.

## NOTES

[6] Daniel Blum, *A Pictorial History of American Theatre: 1860–1976*, rev. 4th ed. (New York: Crown Publishers, 1977), 27.

[7] Catalog, *The Great Scene Painting Studios of the Sosman and Landis Co.* (Chicago: n.d.), 3.

The following disclaimer appeared in the 1889 Sosman and Landis catalog. "CAUTION. Our prices on scenery invariably come in competition with some so-called 'Scenic Studios,' the *Local Fresco Artists* and *Sign Painters*. All are emphatic in stating their ability to paint Scenery as good as the best. *The utter absurdity of such statements should be apparent at a glance.*

We expect competition, but such parties *are not worthy competitors,* and *it is impossible* that they should in any degree equal the *artistic* and *correct scenery* made by us with our corps of skilled artists—many of whom have held positions as *chief artists* in the *best theatres in the country. . .*

We are in receipt of numerous letters from Hall owners who have entrusted work to irresponsible pretenders, much to their regret and loss.

[8] *Semi-Annual Reunion Program* (Chicago Scottish Rite Bodies: Oct. 8–10, 1884), 6. From the Library of the House of the Temple, Washington D. C. In various catalogs produced by the Sosman and Landis Studios, the founding of the company is listed as either 1875 or 1879. The earlier date probably represents the forming of the company by stage employees of Chicago's opera houses, and the later date is the year of incorporation.

[9] Ibid.

[10] Robert G. Cole, "Ancient Accepted Scottish Rite Valley of Chicago: 1857–1959," *Chicago Scottish Rite Magazine* (Chicago: April 1957), 96.

[11] *Fall Reunion Program* (Little Rock: Oct. 4–7, 1898), n.p. From the archives of the Albert Pike Memorial Cathedral, Little Rock, AR.

[12] Alvin E. Morris, *To Shine in Use: A Centennial Celebration of the Scottish Rite Bodies of Wichita, Kansas* (Wichita Scottish Rite: 1986), 27.

[13] Ibid., 12.

[14] Frank A. Derr, "Chronicles of Oklahoma Scottish Rite Masonry," *The Oklahoma Consistory* (Oklahoma Scottish Rite: Feb. 1949), 11.

[15] James D. Carter, *History of the Supreme Council 33o — 1891–1921* (Washington D.C.: Supreme Council, 1971), 167.

[16] See note 11.

[17] *Spring Reunion Program* (Little Rock: May 16–18, 1904), n.p. From the archives of the Albert Pike Memorial Cathedral, Little Rock, AR.

[18] Morris, 28–30.

[19] *The Scottish Rite Temple* (Guthrie Scottish Rite Temple Commemorative Pamplet: n.d.), 2.

[20] Thomas Moses, *My Diary* (unpublished manuscript: 1932), 59. With the John R. Rothgeb Papers, Theatre Arts Collection, Harry Ranson Humanities Research Center, University of Texas, Austin. Used with permission of Mrs. Doris Moses Finke, granddaughter of Thomas Moses and donor of this manuscript.

[21] Ibid., 53.

[22] Hugo Volland (Volland and Toomey), William Knox Brown (Twin City Scenic Company), Llemuel Graham (Kansas City Scenic), and Edgar L. Gossage (Great Western Stage Equipment Company) were all active Masons.

[23] M.V. Scott, "The Stage—Scenically," *Billboard* (Dec. 10, 1921), 83.

[24] Ibid.

[25] Moses, 84.

[26] Letter to John R. Rothgeb from John Hanny, scenic artist for Sosman and Landis. With the John R. Rothgeb Papers, Theatre Arts Collection, Harry Ranson Humanities Research Center, University of Texas, Austin.

FIG · 1

A combined wind, thunder, and rain machine from the Ward-Stilson Co.'s *Catalogue for the Independent Order of Odd Fellows #43* (Anderson, IN: 1911). Courtesy of the Library of the Museum of Our National Heritage, Lexington, MA

*The sound representations are much more realistic than can be produced by the hand apparatus sold by others. The wind effect is wonderfully real, and at will you can produce anything from a murmuring breeze to a cyclone. The other sound devices are just as effective.*

*By the manipulation of levers you can produce any one sound without the others, or a combination of any two of them, or all three at once as you may desire.*
*$11.75*

FIG · 2

A flash torch from C. E. Ward's *Catalogue for the Improved Order of Red Men #114* (New London, OH: 1923).

*Lightning Boxes, made of tin with alcohol lamp in center; a compartment made to hold lycopodium powder with a tube attachment for blowing powder over the flame, thus causing the flash; all complete including a pound of lycopodium $5.00*

Description of a similar stage effect created by Henderson-Ames and available to Scottish Rite Bodies in 1896. Henderson-Ames Co.'s *Catalogue for the Ancient and Accepted Scottish Rite #148* (Kalamazoo, MI: 1896).

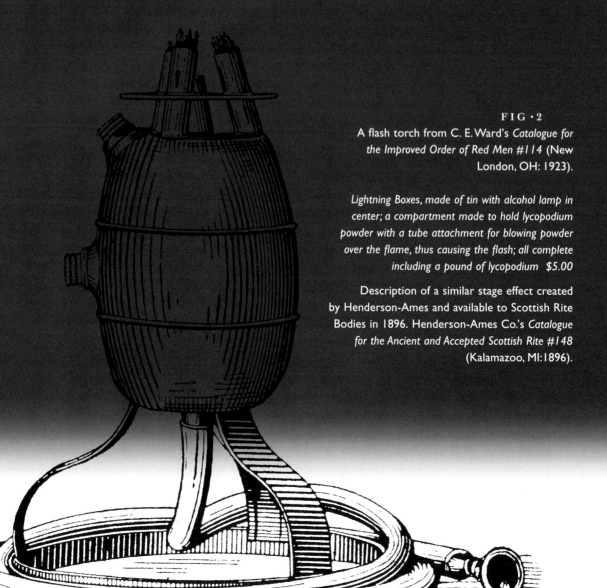

**L A W R E N C E   J .   H I L L**

# D R A M A T I C   I N I T I A T I O N

**T**HE LATE NINETEENTH AND EARLY TWENTIETH CENTURIES SAW NUMEROUS TECHNICAL INNOVATIONS AND ILLUSIONARY EFFECTS ALTER THE STAGING OF AMERICAN POPULAR ENTERTAINMENT—IN THE LEGITIMATE THEATRE AND IN BALLET AND OPERA, VARIETY AND VAUDEVILLE, AND EXPOSITIONS AND FAIRS SUCH AS THE 1893 COLUMBIAN EXPOSITION IN CHICAGO AND THE 1904 LOUISIANA PURCHASE EXPOSITION IN ST. LOUIS. The possibilities presented by the introduction of electricity were, in large part, the impetus to improve staging. But even more important was the need to attract an audience in an increasingly competitive market. This heightened interest in visual and auditory stimulation at the turn of the century parallels the introduction and incorporation of these same devices in the Scottish Rite of Freemasonry.

Initially, most fraternities that emerged in the last half of the nineteenth century made only limited use of visual and auditory effects. Eventually, however, such basic contrivances as the wind machine and the thunder sheet were incorporated in the groups' more elaborate rituals (FIG. 1). Members first constructed these simple mechanical devices in imitation of similar apparatuses used on the popular stage. Although extremely crude compared with today's stage and theatre technology, these devices provided a sense of verisimilitude and atmosphere appropriate to the specific locations indicated in the rituals (FIG. 2).

The dramatic and religious content of many of the rituals—the story of David and Goliath for the Independent Order of Odd Fellows, the Damon and Pythias fable for the Knights of Pythias, and the Hiram legend for Freemasonry—provided opportunities for increasing these effects both to engage new members and to allow current members to participate as actors and as backstage technicians. During the last half of the nineteenth century, most fraternal organizations began to move away from the written word, communicated originally in an aural tradition, to a more visual and realistic enactment of these various rituals. The first step in this process was the use of a tracing board, or chart, displaying various symbols and Victorian iconography central to the moral lessons of each fraternity's degrees (FIG. 3). These simple teaching devices were used to instruct a candidate on the important symbols described within a degree.

Before long, the magic lantern and photographic slides, both popular-entertainment devices, were supplanting the tracing board. [1] The oil magic lantern was one of the first tools used to transform a lodge room into another location for the edification of the members (FIG. 4). In fact, the Independent Order of Odd Fellows, the Junior Order of United American Mechanics, and all branches of Freemasonry including the Blue Lodge, American Rite, Scottish Rite, and Order of the Eastern Star projected glass slides in order to instruct new members. [2]

By the turn of the century, fraternal-supply catalogs reflected myriad sources of illumination, the changing technology, and the range of commercial and economic choices available for

**FIG · 3**

A degree chart for the Independent Order of Odd Fellows, with the primary symbols and icons that are depicted in the rituals of the four degrees, from the Henderson-Ames Co.'s *Catalogue for the Independent Order of Odd Fellows* (Kalamazoo, MI:1910). Courtesy of the Library of the Museum of National Heritage, Lexington, MA

the lodge; these mirrored the range of stage effects found in the scenic supply catalogs, with a choice of costs and quality of good, better, and best. Among the options were crude-oil projectors and electric projectors using carbon arc, as well as filament light sources, alternating current or direct current, and single-image or double-image projectors with mechanical or electrical dimmers to cross fade, superimposing one image over another (FIGS. 5, 6). According to the fraternal catalogs, suppliers would provide all types of light sources to meet the needs of any location, whether or not electrical service was available. [5]

A new visual device, the stereopticon, was used in fraternal initiation and instruction to simulate both motion and transformation (FIG. 7). For example, slides used in progression demonstrated a Christ figure ascending into the clouds or transformed a scenic location from day to night. With technical development, the projector evolved from a device of simple instruction to an illusionary tool that heightened the message of ritual and the emotional experience of the initiate (FIGS. 8–10). The progression from tracing board to projected image clearly demonstrated the quest for a means to enlarge the image and move from a symbolic to a more literal or realistic representation. Another advance in this direction was the addition of specialized cabinets. As a precursor to the fraternal stage, these provided a mechanized transformation incorporating lighting and small-scale painted images (FIG. 11).

### *Lighting the Scottish Rite Stage*

The incorporation and integration of scenery, lighting, and illusionary effects were the final steps the Scottish Rite of Freemasonry took to create the mise-en-scène for the fraternal experience. In 1896 general theatrical staging reflected the centuries-old form of wing-and-drop scenery illuminated by broad, smooth washes of soft light. (See Brockman, FIGS. 7–12.) From the Renaissance on, the scenic artist was responsible for creating, with a brush and paint, the illusion of light—shadows, shafts of dappled sun or soft moonlight, and environmental lighting—on the backdrops and wings. With gas as the source of illumination, lighting devices were placed parallel to the painted scenery, and it was possible to crudely adjust the intensity of lighting with a gas table or to subtly change the color through mechanical devices.

While many ingenious staging innovations can be attributed to the Industrial Revolution, the one that most transformed the stage was the introduction of electric light, at the Munich Exhibition of Electricity in 1883, to replace the romantic gaslight of the Victorian era [4] (FIGS. 12, 13). The first electrical lighting instruments were similar to the gas fixtures but with an improved source, which cast more light on participants and scenery and, not inconsequentially, reduced fire

*112*

Virtue, Truth and Honor are the three most essential qualities of a Knight. A true Knight must be willing to die in defense of Truth and Honor.

### FIG · 4

An oil magic lantern from the Henderson-Ames Co.'s *Catalogue for the Ancient and Accepted Scottish Rite #148* (Kalamazoo, MI:1896).

*The "Excelsior" Sciopticon, with patent three wick lamp, which gives a uniform illustrated field up to twelve feet in diameter, four inch plano-convex condensing lenses, mounted in brass, spring clip for holding carrier with slide, has fine "anchromatic objective," with a rack and pinion adjustment for focus, packed in Russia iron case, which can be used as a stand for lantern: supply of glasses, wicks, funnels and can for lamp including screen. $30.00*

### FIG · 5

"The Leader Magic Lantern" retained the basic optical components of the oil lantern and substituted an electric lamp as the source. From the M. C. Lilley Co.'s *Catalogue for the Chapters of Royal Arch Masons #157* (Columbus, OH: 1908).

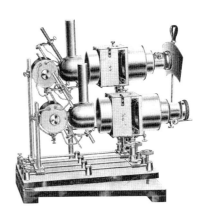

### FIG · 6

"The New Century Magic Lantern" substitutes an arc electric system for an incandescent light-bulb for the gas source, providing "improved" illumination. From the M. C. Lilley Co.'s *Catalogue for the Chapter of Royal Arch Masons #157* (Columbus, OH: 1908).

*There can be no brighter nor more intense and concentrated light than the Ninety Degree hand-feed electric arc light. It is built upon entirely new lines, compact in size and the feeding mechanism being operated from the rear permits its use in almost any sized magic lantern body without reconstructing the body . . .*

*Organizations owning a magic lantern with an inferior light and having the advantage of an electric current, can purchase this lamp with all confidence in its proving highly satisfactory. Particulars upon application. . . .*

*Price, including our combined operating and carrying case, a rheostat, a knife switch and a screen twelve feet square. $80.40*

### FIG · 7

The "Dissolving Arc Lantern" provided two projectors with a "dissolving" baffle or shutter that allowed the operator to superimpose two images. As the shutter blocked one projector, the other produced a clear image, and the second projector could then receive another slide. The crude manipulation or cross fading of the glass-slide images produced a sense of motion unequaled in the single-projector process. "With dissolving shutter," this unit cost $345. From the Henderson-Ames Co.'s *Catalogue for the Ancient and Accepted Scottish Rite #148* (Kalamazoo, MI: 1896).

30TH DEGREE • KNIGHT KADOSH

We learn that Knowledge is Power. Little can be expected of an ignorant man. He is always the dupe of the artful and cunning. The well informed man on

FIGS · 8–10

These three glass slides demonstrate the progression of slides moving from a cloud-filled image to partial clearing to a distant castle in ruins. Courtesy of the Scottish Rite Bodies of Minneapolis, MN

FIG · 11

This pictorial scene depicts the location indicated in the second degree of the ritual for the Independent Order of Odd Fellows. From the Henderson-Ames Co.'s *Catalogue for the Independent Order of Odd Fellows #5* (Kalamazoo, MI:1910s). Courtesy of the Library of the Museum of Our National Heritage, Lexington, MA

He is neither True Knight or True man who is unfaithful to his word in any of the transactions of life, public or private.

The Changing Light of Dramatic Initiation

FIG · 12
An illustration of the Munich Exhibition of
Electricity, *Scientific American Supplement*
(Nov. 1883).

hazards. Subsequent improvements in filament technology increased the intensity of the light and allowed greater color saturation of the scene; lighting could now create a changing night sky or complement the locale and atmosphere depicted by the scenery. Eventually, the effectiveness of the illusion produced by electrical lighting diminished the significance of the illusion created by the scenic artist; the result was an aesthetic break with nineteenth-century tradition and the Victorian sensibility.

Between 1896 and 1929, the fraternal stage reflected the vast changes that were occurring in stage lighting for popular entertainment. The earliest Scottish Rite installations (most still equipped today as when they were installed) illustrate turn-of-the-century staging practices and the interrelationship of scenery, lighting, and stage effects. Scenic artists provided the basic composition and created the illusion of light with paint, while border lights in three colors—red, blue, and white—produced atmospheric effects and suggested the time of day when a scene occurred. With mechanical dimmers it was easier to control more precisely the intensity of the lighting so it could reflect the changing mood of the ritual text.

Both popular-theatre venues and the Scottish Rite membership relied on the same suppliers, who supported the latter with the needed expertise while providing specifications and installation guides. For example, a detailed 1910 contract between the Masons of Guthrie, Oklahoma, and the M. C. Lilley Company called for "a Cutler-Hammer dimmer plant, a marble switchboard, five 25' border rows (to be placed overhead of the scenery) wired to burn three colors and eight ground row lights, each holding 21 lamps for three color control, plus additional 'bunch lights,' stage pockets for plugging into the system, and related equipment." The cost for this lighting was $2676.30[5] (FIG. 14).

In a 1904 issue of the *New Age* magazine, Charles E. Rosenbaum describes the perceived impact of this stage paraphernalia on the second temple in Little Rock: "It is claimed and we do not doubt that it is true, that the stage equipment in Little Rock is the most perfect in America—not only for Masonic purposes, for which it is used exclusively, but from any other point of view . . . nowhere else in America, with the possible exception of one theatre in New York, and one in Chicago, is it possible to produce either the scene or electric effects that can be produced on this stage."[6]

The lighting, Rosenbaum continues, was "handled with great effect and with precision of beauty through the medium of a specially designed switchboard, the creation of Brother Bestor G. Brown."[7] A growing interest in such innovative theatrical staging attracted many brethren to the Little Rock temple "for the purpose of observing its excellent arrangement and equipment and using them in other buildings."[8]

Although elaborate lighting and stage effects were being used in Scottish Rite rituals across the United States, the nineteenth-century tradition of wing-and-drop scenery remained consistent. New Scottish Rite theatres were built with fly lofts above the stage and rigged for 60 to 120 cut

FIG·13

A series of knobs on the gas table controlled
the intensity by limiting the amount of gas burned
by the variety of individual lighting devices.
Courtesy of the John R. Rothgeb Papers, Theatre
Arts Collection, Harry Ransom Humanities Research
Center, University of Texas, Austin

FIG·14

Lighting instruments used at the turn of the century demonstrate the various mechanical
devices available to change color and to "bunch"
light sources together for increased intensity.
Albert A. Hopkins, ed. and comp., *Magic:
Stage Illusions and Scientific Diversions, Including Trick
Photography* (New York: Munn & Co., 1911).

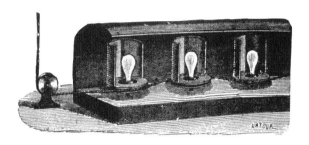

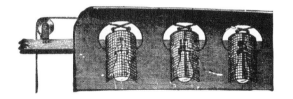

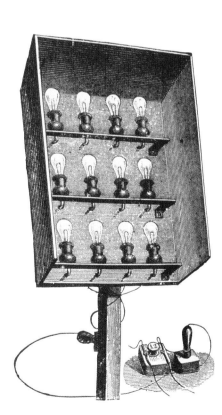

The Changing Light of Dramatic Initiation

**FIGS · 15–17**

To demonstrate the potential of lighting with the scenery, small electrified stages were constructed by the studios. Sosman and Landis assembled this one for use with a collection of sketches produced in the late 1920s. Figure 16 shows the twenty-first degree as colored by the sketch artist, while figure 17 demonstrates the color shift possible with stage lighting as demonstrated in the model stage. Courtesy of the John R. Rothgeb Papers, Harry Ransom Humanities Research Center, University of Texas, Austin

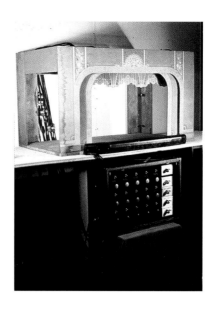

FIG · 18
A backstage view of a translucent panel and the revelation of the secret word in the popular-entertainment theatre.

*A rather curious illusion occurs in* Don Juan. *The monument of the Gubernator bears the inscription, "Here revenge awaits the murderer." The moment that Don Juan appears in front of the monument, one of the stage hands removes a strip of some opaque substance from behind the transparent inscription, which now appears in brilliant letters on the [front of the] base of the monument; the letters being lighted by lamps behind the statue.*

Albert A. Hopkins, ed. and comp., *Magic: Stage Illusions and Scientific Diversions, Including Trick Photography* (New York: Munn & Co., 1911).

drops and backdrops; now, however, part of the design "package" was also state-of-the-art electric lighting. The interrelationship of the lighting with the scenery required that each element (backdrop, cut drop, and border light) be installed according to a prescribed formula that all temples built between 1896 and 1929 had to follow (FIGS. 15–17).

To accommodate the formula for installation of the Scottish Rite stage that mimicked the approach of professional stock companies, fraternal suppliers developed a system of guides, or "cheat books," that enabled novice stagehands in communities everywhere to put on "professional" presentations. The books provided specifications for the selected cut drops, wings, and backdrops that were to be lowered, or "flown in," from the loft, suggested setups for lighting including mood and color, and directed the placement of all properties for each scene of the various degrees.

### Effects: Creating the Total Experience

Just as theatrical lighting evolved from gas and oil to electricity, so did stage effects. One of the earliest effects featured in Scottish Rite rituals and those of other fraternities was the revelation of a secret word. This was originally achieved using a transparency box that had interchangeable front panels of silk. The trick was to light this translucent fabric from behind with a candle, oil, or gas so that the auspicious word, painted translucent on the back of the panel, seemed to appear magically in the darkened lodge room (FIG. 18). With the introduction of electric lighting and sophisticated scenery, the same device was employed, but now the secret word or symbol, skillfully painted into the scenery, could impressively emerge from the center of a rock or the lintel in a peristyle on the front of the backdrop (FIGS. 19A, B).

Two spectacular effects vividly illustrate the cross-fertilization of theatrical technique with Scottish Rite ritual. The first involved a device that was the precedent of a current pop-culture item, the light saber of the *Star Wars* trilogy. Figure 20, an illustration from Albert A. Hopkins's *Magic: Stage Illusions and Scientific Diversions, Including Trick Photography* (1911), demonstrates the use of electrified swords that spark when placed in close contact. The aural and visual impact of swordplay transported the audience beyond mundane reality and into the imaginative, intensified world of the ritual. Scottish Rite leaders recognized the power of this effect on those experiencing initiatory rituals. The set of dueling swords pictured in figure 21 is still used in St. Louis.

The second elaborate special effect is known as Pepper's Ghost, or the Blue Room.[9] Patented in England in the 1860s, this illusion was designed to illustrate the mortality of mankind by "revealing" on a so-called exemplar, a member of the initiation class, the ravages of death (FIG. 22). The trick depended upon the use of a skeleton, controlled lighting, and a piece of plate glass to show the audience the exemplar slowly stripped of his flesh and revealed in skeletal form. The effect compress-

**FIGS · 19 A – B**
The Peristyle with the use of light boxes to
reveal the secret words. Courtesy of the Scottish
Rite Bodies of Asheville, NC

**FIG · 20**
Image of an "electrical duel" used in *Faust* at the
Metropolitan Opera.

*The duel takes place at a part of the stage where two
plates of copper are sunk into the flooring. These
plates are connected with the electric current. Copper
nails are driven into one shoe of Valentine and one
shoe of Faust, and the wires are run up their bodies to
the swords. When they draw their swords they
insert the wire into the hilts by means of a plug; they
are connected to the copper plate. Every time
Mephistopheles interposes the sword and strikes up
the contending weapons, which are in contact, the
sparks fly furiously and the weird crackling sounds are
heard as in lightning.*

Albert A. Hopkins, ed. and comp., *Magic:
Stage Illusions and Scientific Diversions, Including Trick
Photography* (New York: Munn & Co., 1911).

To fall and rise aga

120

Theatre of the Fraternity

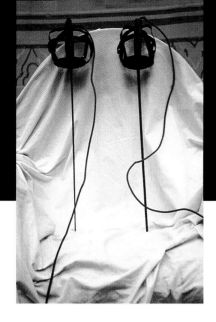

heroic than by greater strength never to fall. To do wrong and make amends, to sin and repent, belongs to a noble nature.

The Changing Light of Dramatic Initiation

FIGS · 23 & 24

Backdrop for the seventeenth degree, or the Volcano
of the Isle of Patmos. The image on the right shows
the panel revealing the visions, or first five seals.

es the viewer's sense of time and space and encourages a willing suspension of disbelief.

Of the various Masonic degrees requiring support from lighting and stage effects, the seventeenth degree is perhaps the most complex and impressive. The story of this ritual is based on a romantic interpretation of the biblical account of the Seven Seals from the books of Revelation to John. On a backdrop created by Sosman and Landis for the Wichita Scottish Rite temple in 1908, a painted mountain and tranquil lake represent the island of Patmos (FIGS. 23, 24). For this blue moon-lit scene, a panel drops down from the front of the tomb on the left to reveal a series of painted images that slide in, one at a time, to represent the first five seals. "When he (the exemplar) opened the sixth seal . . . there was a great earthquake . . . and the full moon became like blood (FIGS. 25, 26)."[10] At this moment, the back of the drop is bathed in red, turning the translucent moon into "blood"; this is followed by a cacophony produced by the rumble trough and a thunder sheet; concurrently, panels flip up from the back of the drop to reveal a volcanic plume over both the mountain and the water; then the opaque shutter is slowly lowered to expose the red back light as rivulets of molten lava cascade down the mountain. These effects, coupled with framed painted pieces of architecture and rock walls that seem to fall apart and collapse on cue, created a visual sensation that impressed the initiates and earned accolades for the responsible stagehands.

### The Emergence of Modernism

The heightened impact of revelation and transformation in the increasingly theatrical initiation of the Scottish Rite paralleled the fraternity's burgeoning membership. Late-Victorian aesthetics, characterized by rich, romantic imagery, were consistent with the language of a melodramatic mid-nineteenth-century ritual. By the early twentieth century, however, staging in the legitimate theatre was changing, as painted two-dimensional scenery was gradually replaced by three-dimensional forms adaptable to improved lighting technology. The earlier washes of gaslight might have been tolerable in the nineteenth-century theatre, but the "bright, directional rays of the electric bulb served to destroy the illusion of two-dimensional scenery."[11]

The scenery, lighting, and stage effects that the Scottish Rite Masons continue to use reflect this dichotomy between a Victorian sensibility and twentieth-century modernism. Because its ritual is best enacted using late-Victorian imagery and enhanced by an archaic use of electric light, the fraternity's staging recalls its origins. As a result, the dramatization of the Scottish Rite still does not fully exploit the lighting and staging advances that distinguish contemporary productions. Granted, certain turn-of-the-century stage lighting and effects continue to inspire a measure of awe today, but they pale by comparison to the illusionary magic of the commercial theatre in, say, New York, London, and Las Vegas, which is now driven by computers and projected holograms.

**FIG · 25**

*He opens the first seal. The organ plays a few notes;
and the V[enerable] M[aster] takes from behind
the organ a bow, a quiver filled with arrows, and a
coronet, and gives them to a Brother and says
to him: "Depart and continue the conquest! And I say,
and lo! a white horse; and he that sat on him held
a bow; and a crown was given unto him: and he went
forth conquering and to conquer.  Open now the
second seal!"*

Albert Pike, *The Magnum Opus or Great Work* (Kila,
MT: Kessinger, 1992; reprinted from the 1857
original).

To teach, you must first learn. To be a soldier of the light, you must first get light. A thing is not just because God wills it; but God

wills it, because it is just. Seek then, first of all, Truth and Justice and the science of knowledge will be given unto you.

The Changing Light of Dramatic Initiation

FIG · 26

*He does so: and the V[enerable] M[aster] takes
from behind the altar a naked sword; [Music is heard
here, and as each seal is opened]; and gives it to
another Brother, saying: "Go forth and create strife and
dissension among the Profane and Wicked, that
they may destroy each other; and smite thou unspar-
ingly the vices, the superstitions and the errors that
infest and inflict the world! For there went out
another horse that was red; and it was given to him
that sat theron to banish peace from the earth,
and that the wicked should slay one another; and
there was given unto him a great sword. Open now the
third seal!" . . . "Open now the sixth seal."*

*He does so: and immediately there is a crash of loud
music from the organ, thunder rolls near the Lodge,
and the lights are now darkened.*

Albert Pike, *The Magnum Opus or Great Work*
(Kila, MT: Kessinger, 1992; reprinted from
the 1857 original).

124

## ⊓ ⊙ T E S

[1] Richard Balzar, *Optical Amusements: Magic Lanterns and Other Transforming Images — A Catalog of Popular Entertainment* (Watertown, MA: Richard Balzar, 1987), 4.

[2] For a comprehensive collection of catalogs from various fraternities and female auxilliaries, see the Library of the Museum of Our National Heritage (MONH) in Lexington, MA.

[3] One catalog from the MONH collection advertised a lantern that would run on a car battery, for use in halls in towns without electricity.

[4] "Illustration of Munich Exhibition of Electricity," *Scientific American Supplement* (Nov. 10, 1883), 6535.

[5] Contract from M. C. Lilley Co. to the board of directors of the Masonic Building Association. From the John R. Rothgeb Papers, Theatre Arts Collection, Harry Ransom Humanities Research Center, University of Texas, Austin.

[6] Charles E. Rosenbaum, "Albert Pike Consistory," *The New Age* (Aug./Sept. 1904), 289.

[7] Ibid., 289. It should be noted that both Rosenbaum and Bestor G. Brown were involved with scenery, lighting, and stage effects. See Brockman essay.

[8] Ibid.

[9] Albert A. Hopkins, ed. and comp., *Magic: Stage Illusions and Scientific Diversions, Including Trick Photography* (New York: Munn & Co., 1911), 320.

[10] Revelation 6.12, *Harper Study Bible*, revised standard version (Grand Rapids, MI: Zondervan Bible Pub., 1988).

[11] A. Nicholas Vardac, *Stage to Screen: Theatrical Methods from Garrick to Griffith* (New York: Benjamin Blom, 1968), 9.

**KENNETH L. AMES** is a historian of American art and material culture with a special interest in the nineteenth century. He is author of *Beyond Necessity: Art in the Folk Tradition* (1977), *Death in the Dining Room and Other Tales of Victorian Culture* (1992), and numerous articles and essays and the editor of decorative-arts bibliographies and books on museology. His current book project is an architectural history of Bishop Street in Honolulu. Ames has lectured widely on folk art, nineteenth-century material culture, Victoriana, and museum issues and has served as a consultant on exhibitions and collections for more than fifty U.S. museums and cultural institutions. On the staff of the Winterthur Museum in Delaware for seventeen years and at the New York State Museum for another five, Ames is currently a free-lance author and consultant based in Niskayuna, New York.

**WILLIAM D. MOORE** is a doctoral candidate in the American and New England Studies Program at Boston University, where he is writing a dissertation about the architecture and material culture of Masonic temples in New York State from 1870 to 1930. He is currently director of the Livingston Masonic Library in New York City.

**MARY ANN CLAWSON** is associate professor of sociology at Wesleyan University and the author of *Constructing Brotherhood: Class, Gender, and Fraternalism* (1989). Her longtime interest in masculinity and popular culture is reflected in current research on gender and rock music, as well as in her studies of the nineteenth-century fraternal movement.

126

**MARK C. CARNES** teaches history at Barnard College, where he also chairs the history department. He wrote *Secret Ritual and Manhood in Victorian America* (1989) and edited, with Clyde Griffen, *Meanings of Manhood: Constructions of Masculinity in Victorian America* (1991) and, with John A. Garraty, *Dictionary of American Biography* (1988). He most recently edited *Past Imperfect: History According to the Movies* (1995) and currently is working on a book on gender and visual perception in Victorian America.

**C. LANCE BROCKMAN** teaches in, and currently chairs, the Department of Theatre and Dance at the University of Minnesota. In 1987 he was curator of "The Twin City Scenic Collection: Popular Entertainment 1895–1929," an exhibition that provided the impetus for "Theatre of the Fraternity." He is currently working on a book that uses principles of historic drawing and painting to teach theatre-design students.

**LAWRENCE J. HILL**, chair of the Department of Communication and Theatre Arts at Western Carolina University, contributed to the "Twin City Scenic" exhibition and co-edited *Opera Houses of the Midwest* (1988). He has designed, lighted, and served as technical director for more than 130 university, community, and dinner-theatre productions.

*127*